(Continued from back cover)

- **"Your statistical department may be interested in knowing that my wife reports that thirteen years of snoring terminated the day after I stopped smoking."** —C. D. M.

- "Twice in the past ten years I have made abortive attempts to stop smoking. My record, until your book came along, was four days. This letter of thanks is being written as I turn into my sixth week of no smoking. It looks as if I made it now! I salute you!"—G. A. W.

- **"I felt I would be remiss if I did not drop you a line to tell you that I just completed a month off the weed after twenty years, thanks only to your volume. I bought six copies and have started a campaign among deserving and needy friends. Would not trade** *How to Stop,* **etc., for a Rosenbach first edition."** —J. J. D., Jr.

- "You may say I am a bit overenthusiastic, but I tell my friends that next to Hamlet your book on *How to Stop Smoking* is the greatest thing ever written. I always thought it was a hopeless struggle, but here I am going into my eighth month, sure I am never going to smoke again. The battle has been won, because I did exactly what you said to do, page by page. You should have at least an honorary chair in applied psychology in one of our universities." —G. W. H., M.D.

HOW TO
STOP
SMOKING

New and revised edition

HERBERT BREAN

PUBLISHED BY POCKET BOOKS NEW YORK

HOW TO STOP SMOKING

Vanguard edition published 1959

Revised, enlarged, and updated POCKET BOOK edition
published January, 1970

Newly revised POCKET BOOK edition
published December, 1975

3rd printing..................December, 1976

This revised POCKET BOOK edition is printed from brand-new
plates made from completely reset, clear, easy-to-read type.
POCKET BOOK editions are published by
POCKET BOOKS,
a division of Simon & Schuster, Inc.,
A GULF+WESTERN COMPANY
630 Fifth Avenue,
New York, N.Y. 10020.
Trademarks registered in the United States
and other countries.

ISBN: 0-671-80213-5.

Front cover design by Milton Charles.
Cover photograph by Carl Kravats.
Printed in the U.S.A.

Contents

A Preface (Which You Can Skip Temporarily As Long As You Come Back to It Later)

AS YOU are about to discover, this book, when it first appeared, began with some portentous words.

"Let the important fact come first: this is a rare book," we trumpeted when we first wrote and published it.

Implausible as it may seem, this author's statement turned out to be fairly correct. It is not merely that *How to Stop Smoking* has sold well. Or that there are more than a million copies in print in twelve foreign languages as well as in English. The rare quality we referred to was that the book was sold with a money-back guarantee: if you did not give up smoking, you got your money back. At last count, something under one hundred readers have demanded a refund.

This has special significance for us personally because it supports our contention that people who *want* to stop smoking *can* do so when they are given proper advice, and that they do not need the presumably stronger incentive resulting from a doctor's warning or a cancer specialist's ominous prognosis.

A striking example of this is afforded by Britain, where the government earlier took a far more drastic stand against smoking, showing anti-smoking films by the hundreds and distributing more than a million bone-chilling posters. Yet British cigarette smoking continued to rise, apparently for the same reason that the British people refused to let Hitler's ruthless bombings in World War II scare them into submission.

You can't permanently frighten people into doing anything. You *can* persuade them by reason, though, and many hundreds of thousands of persons, who have approached the problem with confidence and a little coaxing, rather than fear or superstitious dread, have stopped smoking, often with unexpected ease.

Not that due warnings about the dangers of smoking have not appeared, as the headlines of the past several years show. Smoking has become a far different problem from what it was at the time this book was first published. Do you realize how great a change has occurred in the public's attitude—that is, in *your* attitude —toward smoking? How great a change in the advertising and even the packaging of cigarettes has taken place? How great a change there has been in the claims made for and against cigarettes?

It was in late 1953 that the American public was jarred out of its tobacco-soothed lethargy by the chilling words of a noted St. Louis surgeon. He was Dr. Evarts A. Graham, who, with young Dr. Ernest L. Wynder, had reproduced cancer in mice experimentally by coating their backs with tars obtained from tobacco smoke. Said Dr. Graham flatly:

"This shows conclusively that there is something in cigarette smoking which can produce cancer. This is no longer merely a possibility. Our experiments have proved it beyond any doubt."

Suddenly the public became aware of something cancer specialists had long known and wondered about: that in the preceding twenty years the United States male death rate from cancer of the lung had quadrupled and the death rate among women had doubled. As a cause of death, lung cancer was increasing faster than any other disease. In the same twenty-year period, cigarette sales in this country had approximately quadrupled.

In the uproar that followed, the tobacco industry took large newspaper advertisements to announce the formation of its Tobacco Industry Research Committee, which would aid "the research effort into all phases of tobacco and health." Critics of the Graham-Wynder results argued that inducing cancer on a mouse's back by painting it with tobacco tars was a far different thing from proving that inhaled tobacco smoke could cause cancer in a human lung. Others pointed out that previous researchers had failed to produce cancer in similar ways; perhaps Drs. Graham and Wynder had merely come up with a "freak" result.

Then in June of 1954 the American Medical Association convened in San Francisco and heard a report from the American Cancer Society on the first half of a projected five-year study of 187,000 men between the ages of 50 and 70. Drs. E. Cuyler Hammond and Daniel Horn, director and assistant director respectively of statistical research for the society, said they had originally planned to publish nothing for at least another year. But, they said, "We found cigarette smokers had so much higher death rates that we didn't think we could withhold the information another year . . . we were thinking of saving lives."

For the Hammond-Horn study embraced more than cancer of the lung. True, they had found, as of the time of this preliminary report, that lung cancer deaths were from three to nine times as common among cigarette smokers as among non-smokers. But they also reported:

The death rate from heart attacks and coronary artery disease was 50 percent higher among cigarette smokers than non-smokers.

Even when lung cancer was excluded from the statistics, the incidence of death from other forms of cancer (kidneys, stomach, intestinal tract) was higher among cigarette smokers than non-smokers.

A year later, Drs. Hammond and Horn reported again to the A.M.A. convention, armed now with another twelve months of study and statistical analyses. The new report buttressed previous findings thus:

Two-packs-a-day smokers had a death rate ninety times as high as non-smokers.

Those who smoked two *or more* packs

a day showed a lung cancer death rate three times that of the one-pack-a-day smoker.

The lung cancer increase was apparent even among those who smoked fewer than ten cigarettes a day.

This was throwing gasoline on an already blazing fire, for the public by now was definitely alarmed. The United States Public Health Service reported in June of 1955 that 1.5 million citizens had given up cigarettes in the previous eighteen months.

One sign of the times was a suit for $250,000 brought by a St. Louis factory worker against four tobacco companies and a grocery chain. In the words of the Associated Press, the plaintiff "said in his petition that he had accepted the defendants' public assurances their respective brands of cigarettes were free from harmful substance." After smoking more than two packs a day for twenty-two years, he was found to be suffering from a lung cancer and had to have a lung removed, which impaired his earning ability and also cost him considerable medical expense. The suit was ultimately dropped, but it was a significant straw in the wind.

So was the announcement by the chief of

California's Bureau of Chronic Diseases that lung cancer, causing more than 22,000 deaths a year, was an epidemic that had not yet reached its peak. So was the cigarette case announced by a famous New York jeweler, with compartments for both cigarettes and the Life Saver mints with which many people were trying to cut down their cigarette smoking.

Meanwhile the cigarette manufacturers fumed and sputtered—and, with some prodding from the Federal Trade Commission, made some major changes in their advertising and packaging. One industry leader charged that the American Cancer Society was out to destroy the tobacco industry, for reasons which were not too clear. But in the main the tobacco industry contented itself with issuing denials that the mounting evidence proved anything at all. Its position was probably epitomized by an earlier statement from a tobacco research chief: "If there really is an element in tobacco that causes cancer, we'd want to know about it ourselves. If it could be proved, there'd be no trick, technically, to eliminating it." This last was at least overly optimistic, since as this is written the cancer-forming agent in tobacco has yet to be isolated, let alone eliminated.

More significant was the change in advertising. Almost overnight there vanished from the

American scene those old familiars: "less injurious tars . . . less throat scratch . . . get a *lift.* . . ." Cigarette advertising became a simple appeal to enjoy flavor and aroma, instead of an invitation to achieve perfect health and eternal youth through smoking. Similarly, cigarette packaging began to stress the clean whites and simple designs and typography associated with sanitation, purity, and science. *Advertising Age* reported that cigarette companies spent 5½ cents per carton to advertise their product in 1956, in contrast to 4 cents in 1955.

It was in June of 1957 that the American Cancer Society, through Drs. Hammond and Horn, submitted its final report on the five-year study of 187,000 subjects. In a sense, it said little that was new. The report stated again that the death rate among cigarette smokers was higher than among non-smokers, and that smokers died at an earlier age. It also observed an "extremely high" association between cigarette smoking and deaths from cancer of the lung and other related areas, as well as from heart disease. At a press conference Drs. Hammond and Horn roughly estimated, on the basis of their figures, that cigarette smoking shortened life expectancy by seven to eight years, cigar smoking by one year to eighteen months, pipe smoking by two to three months.

Both cigarette smokers before they began their study, they were both now converted to pipes.

Then in 1964 came the crushing report of the committee of the U.S. Surgeon General which, having made its own independent survey of all the responsible studies made by other authorities, declared flatly that cigarette smoking contributed so greatly to the American death rate, that "appropriate remedial action" was required.

Sales of filter-tipped cigarettes, already on the rise, began to boom because many smokers believed that filters protect one against the injurious tars in tobacco smoke, "tars" being a catch-all word for the solids, usually hydrocarbons, in the smoke. Actually, no filter does this with 100 percent effectiveness, and some filters pass as much tar to the smoker as does the corresponding "straight," or filter-less, cigarette.

Indeed, the Federal Trade Commission's regularly issued test results on the tar and nicotine content of popular brands show that a filter-tip cigarette can deliver as much as 30 milligrams of tar and 1.6 milligrams of nicotine to its smoker. Filters are uncertain things; sometimes a non-filter cigarette delivers fewer of the injurious substances than does its filter-tip counterpart.* Perhaps the most that can be said for filters is that there seems some reason to believe their users cough less.

While tobacco smoke, or the tars or nicotine therein, has yet to be pathologically *proven* a major cause of lung cancer, increased incidence of heart disease and other ills, the statistical correlation between heavy smoking and dying from these is overwhelming. And the studies that have been made have turned up some other interesting corollaries and leads:

Apparently the tobacco substance that causes the lung cancer is a slow-working material, since it affects men mostly in middle and later life—from the late forties to seventy, approximately—who have smoked heavily for years.

Women are less prone to lung cancer than men—at the moment. This is apparently due to the fact that women have not been as consistent or as heavy smokers as men over the years. But since women are now smoking much more heavily than they used to, the lung cancer incidence among

---

* Apparently because the manufacturer uses stronger tobacco in them to compensate for the filtered-out taste.

women can be expected to increase sharply in the next couple of decades. In fact, the increase is already observable.

Both cigars and pipes—especially pipes —are far safer than cigarettes.

The more heavily you smoke cigarettes, the more likely you are to develop cancer or heart disease. If you stop completely, the greater your chances of not contracting these diseases.

Whether you live in the country or the city doesn't seem to make much difference. It has been argued that the pall of carbon monoxide, oil fumes, and coal dust surrounding a city may be as cancer-causing as cigarette smoke. But the Hammond-Horn study covered thousands of both city and rural residents. The difference in death rates between the two was microscopic. The difference between the smokers' and non-smokers' death rates was enormous.

All of which leaves us where?
Scared to death? Well, as the author of a

book rather deliberately designed not to scare anyone, we hope not. For we happen to believe that you can never scare, or bully or bludgeon, anyone into doing anything useful or constructive. So, having taken cognizance of the cancer scare, please, as you read on, dismiss it from your mind for the time being. We are *not* going to frighten you into anything!

We admire the scientists who have discovered what tobacco smoke seems to do to people. We think that the people who did the statistical work: the Hammonds and Horns and their thousands of assistants (and thousands they had)—and the people who are doing the laboratory work—the Grahams and Ochsners and especially the Wynders—and the Surgeon General's experts—all deserve an enormous vote of thanks from the very people whom they have made uneasy.

But we also think, as we said, that in the last analysis very few people are going to be frightened out of smoking. They should be—of course. But they won't be.

There is another motive that can stop them, though. It is the one on which this book was originally postulated.

Remember what we said? This book appeared in 1951, which was long before anyone except the medical people had an inkling of what was coming. And even to them it was only an inkling. In spite of that, the book helped a lot of people to stop smoking, and it did this without threats.

The point is that you either want to stop smoking or you don't. If you don't want to stop, forget all this.

Stop here.

But if you *want* to stop, consider you have in your hand an instrument that many thousands of other people have found effective. (We have the mail to prove it, and you will presently read some of it.)

All we ask of you is that you do *want* to stop. Ignore the cancer scare if you will, ignore the heart ailments, forget everything except the one simple fact that you want deeply to give up smoking.

Then you read this book and do what it tells you to do, and you will stop. That was true almost two decades ago. It has been true ever since.

And it will still be true in 19?? when science may have isolated the dangerous element in tobacco and developed a way to eliminate it without affecting tobacco flavor.

For, as you are about to find out, the reasons for wanting not to smoke go deeper than fear, and the pleasures and satisfaction of successfully giving it up are far greater than any mere alleviation of sudden panic.

That is a fact that has never been properly emphasized.

HERBERT BREAN

1

Just as a matter of record

LET the important fact come first: this is a rare book. It is really sold with a money-back guarantee. Here is the guarantee:

If you *want* to give up smoking—that is, if you have said to yourself, or to your wife, or to friends over the past several years, "Gosh, I'd like to give these things up, but I know I can't. . . ."

If that is the case, and you will read this book through and put its precepts into practice . . .

It is *guaranteed* that you will give up smoking.

If you don't, you get your money back, and no questions asked.

As a matter of fact there is an additional guarantee: it isn't even a hard book to read. On the contrary, it's easy. Because it concerns a problem that has been bothering you for a long time, a problem that has bothered you both mentally and physically, and it points the solution for you.

It is written by someone who has been all the way through the nicotine habit and is thoroughly familiar with the well-known pleasures of smoking and the little-known, but very real, pleasures of non-smoking. Not a crank, not a solemn moralizer, not a guy who presently will flash livid pictures of a smoker's lungs or stomach on a screen and scare the dickens out of you.

Rather, a guy who has smoked cigarette, cigar, and pipe by turns, has a nice collection of fifteen-dollar briars (now gathering dust), and has touched a match to, and inhaled, some three to four hundred thousand cigarettes.

So please don't be alarmed. Wistfully, perhaps almost hopelessly, you *want* to give up smoking. Well, you *can*.

If you read on, you *will*.

That's guaranteed. You have nothing to lose but your chain-smoking.

Why not try it?

2

Why you should not give up smoking

THIS book is addressed primarily to heavy smokers, whether of cigars, cigarettes, or pipe. The person who smokes one cigar, or four or five cigarettes a day, has no real problem. He might be a little better off without this mild indulgence, but unless he is in exceptionally poor health, or has an abnormally low tolerance for tobacco, he does not need to put a stop to it. Indeed, his doctor may very well approve of it on the ground that, everything considered, the relaxation his smoking affords him does more good than harm.

But let's not kid ourselves. That kind of smoker is in the minority. As this is written, the United States is smoking cigarettes alone at the rate of about 1.5 billion a day. That means 210 packs a year for everyone eighteen years old and over in the country. Nor even to think of the cigar and pipe smokers!

Since roughly 25 percent of that population does not smoke at all, it appears that the average smoker consumes cigarettes at the rate of about seven packs a week. That is the *average*. Anyone with ordinary business or social associations knows that one and one-half to three packs is the *daily* allotment of a great many smokers.

And that is dangerously too much, for reasons which we will presently examine.

But before we begin going into such fascinating questions as *why* you smoke, or why tobacco has gradually acquired so overpowering a hold on so much of the population, or why it is virtually a national superstition to believe that you cannot stop smoking—that is, before beginning to explore the basic nature of the enemy we are presently going to attack— let's pause, like any smart field general, to survey the enemy's strength and note the disposition of his forces.

That is, let's start by asking why should you want to give up smoking at all?

For there are many good reasons why you

should not, and until you examine them all, take them into full account and acknowledge their validity, you will be in a psychologically defensive position. You will be like a man trying to free himself from the embrace of an octopus without even knowing how many arms it has.

So just sit back comfortably, please, and, if you will be so obliging, light up a cigarette. Or a cigar. Or a pipe. Go through the whole ritual, too. If it's a cigarette, tamp the end lovingly so that you get a good light and no tobacco fragments reach your tongue and spoil the pleasure of your smoke. Light it carefully, too, getting no sulphur fumes from the match or gasoline fumes from the lighter. (The best way is to hold the cigarette *above* the flame, not in it. That way makes it most fragrant.) Sit back and draw in the first savory lungful, before you go on reading.

Tastes pretty good, doesn't it?

It sure does. So why give it up?

Why, indeed?

Maybe before you have finished this chapter you will want another. Have it, by all means. Smoke all you want. For if you get through this chapter and at the end of it still want to give up smoking, a big part of your battle—a battle which takes not merely preparation and intelligent execution but a sort of psychological conditioning—will be won.

So, as you enjoy your smoke, let's consider why you should put yourself to the mental anguish and physical torment of depriving yourself of something you enjoy.

Are there any really valid reasons why you should give up smoking? Certainly there are plenty why you should not. After all, you're not getting any younger. The number of pleasures left in life is slowly but steadily diminishing. Maybe you can't eat all the things you used to. Maybe the same is true of drinking. Sooner or later, your interest in the opposite sex is going to become largely academic; maybe it has already. If you are between thirty-five and fifty or so, the needs of your family or the exigencies of your business may cut in on your leisure or vacations; possibly you can't afford the money or the time for golf or fishing trips, or night clubs, or serious reading, or beer parties, or postgraduate studies, or whatever else you might like.

But in this changing and aging world smoking seems to be a constant. It is enjoyed by old men and young, by high-school girls and dowagers, by corncob-puffing crones who are interviewed in the papers on the occasion of their reaching the age of one hundred, and

Why You Should **Not** Give Up Smoking

by—in one case at least—babies of fourteen months. You may remember the news stories when a fourteen-month-old baby who smoked cigars came to public notice. He's still alive and smoking, at last report.

Not only does the pleasure of tobacco span all ages but it is one pleasure which is not expensive nor obviously—since you've been doing it for a long time and are still alive—unhealthful or debilitating. Through many a tense business conference, long nocturnal vigil, or uneasy social affair, a cigarette (many cigarettes!) have seen you through. A flash of the match, a long, deep inhalation, then the welcome, soothing fragrance—and somehow you feel better.

Why give that up?

Smoking is a solace in moments of depression. It is a pleasant companion in work or play. It is an anodyne during sleepless nights. It is "something to do with your hands" when entertaining a guest or business contact; it affords you an opportunity for graciously offering hospitality in the form of a cigarette or cigar. Most of all, it makes possible thirty or fifty or sixty separate and pleasant "treats" or acts of self-indulgence which you can give yourself every day. Life at best is often a pretty grim bit of business, containing all too few pleasures. Why deny yourself these frequent little pleasures?

That is, why give up smoking?

It's all right to say you should cut down. Probably you should. But you'll get around to it sooner or later. You know you need not smoke as much as you do around the office, say, or on the job, at the bridge table, or while working around the house.

But that first cigarette after breakfast, or even the first one when you get up—those are the ones you can't give up. They're just too darned pleasant! And why should you?

After all, the doctors can't seem to decide whether smoking is harmful or not.* While working on this book, we did considerable delving into the medical records of one of the country's largest medical libraries. We found there are reports in medical journals which can prove almost anything anyone might want to prove about smoking. The doctors can't make up their minds about smoking's long-term effects on your throat, for example. Or on your lungs. Or on the length of your life. Or whether, even, there is such a thing as a cigarette cough. There seems to be a correlation between heavy smoking and cancer of the lung—but whether

---

* This was in 1951, of course!

it is the *smoking* that causes the *cancer* is something else again.

You go to your own doctor for a physical examination, and he tells you that you're in pretty good shape, all things considered, although you really ought to cut down on your smoking. You shake your head guiltily and agree, and promise that you will try to. You mean it, too. Then the doctor says, "Well, that's that," and you both take out cigarettes, and when he lights yours for you, you notice that his right forefinger is yellowed by nicotine. Presently you depart, happy in the knowledge that you are in pretty good shape, and confident that if smoking was *really* very bad for you, the doctor wouldn't be doing it himself. And, anyway, you're going to cut down.

So why give it up completely?

If that isn't enough, you can take your choice of the many brands of cigarettes which advertise the statements of "leading medical authorities" who have found that the given cigarettes contain no throat irritants, are "definitely milder," or are "cooler smoking." After all, those people know what they're talking about, don't they?

So what the hell!

Look at the rot that has been published about the evils of tobacco. That it ruins your will power, or causes crime, or drives you insane. You know that's silly! Then look at the people who smoke—the authors and scientists, the business leaders and actors, the athletes and beautiful models.

If that isn't enough, think what famous men have said about tobacco. "Divine, rare, super-excellent," Robert Burton called it. "For thy sake, tobacco," said Charles Lamb, "I would do anything but die." Byron termed it "sublime," and Bulwer-Lytton felt that "A good cigar is as great a comfort to a man as a good cry to a woman." Indeed, said he, "The man who smokes, thinks like a sage and acts like a Samaritan." And Kipling's "A woman is only a woman, but a good cigar is a smoke," is almost too well known to need repeating.

Matter of fact, there's another reason why you shouldn't even *consider* the possibility of your stopping smoking. Not only is it a pleasant, soothing experience in a world whose pleasures are constantly diminishing; it is importantly associated with many other pleasures. One is drinking. If you like an occasional drink or a sociable several drinks, smoking is a wonderful complement to alcohol. Indeed, you may well ask how you could get through a cocktail party without a cigarette's tart flavor to cut through the heavier taste of Manhattans,

Scotch, or even beer. Or there's eating. How good a cigarette is with the coffee after a good dinner! And how necessary!

Give up smoking, and you give up all that. Also, you give up the gold-plated lighter you're so proud of, and which you have brought to such a peak of efficiency that you can win bets with it. Not to mention your several cigarette cases. Or, it may be, the cigar clipper that adds a note of efficient and prosperous dignity to your watch chain. Or the pipes which you have collected over the years and have lovingly buffed and polished to soft, gleaming beauty, or treated like some medieval alchemist with rum or sherry. Give them all up? And what of the expensive humidors on desk or library table? Perhaps you take a little pride in your taste for exotic Turkish blended cigarettes, English pipe mixtures, cigarette holders, or onyx ashtrays. Are you going to throw all these in the trash barrel?

Why should you? Are you crazy? Take this book back and get your money. Forget it! You can't give up smoking!

Another thing. Talk to any friend who is a smoker about the possibility of giving it up completely and he'll probably tell you that *he* cannot do it and wouldn't even dare try. Why? Because any real smoker's physique over the years has grown accustomed to smoking and to what it does for him. Stop smoking—straight off, just like that—and you throw a tremendous strain on your nervous system. Why, you could make a nervous wreck of yourself, he'll tell you. He's seen it happen.

Why risk not only discomfort and unhappiness but the wrecking of your health?

As you can see, there's very little point in giving up smoking. It's a deep, lasting pleasure that appeals to your senses of taste, sight, smell, and touch; a really clean, innocuous sort of "vice"; a practice which is winning wider social acceptance all the time; a bond between good fellows and/or chic women; a habit which carries in its train many other little pleasures.

Give all this up? Don't be silly!

Take this book back where you bought it and get your money back right now. Do it now, before you weaken and start reading the next chapter!

Spend the money on a few mild Havanas or enough cigarettes to get you through tomorrow, or on a new tobacco pouch.

Or on a movie or anything else. But forget about giving up smoking! Maybe some few people can do it, but it would be really rough for you. Too tough. And why should you?

Why You Should **Not** Give Up Smoking

You're going to go on smoking the rest of your life. You're a smoker. That's that. Might as well face up to it.

Pretty convincing, eh?

Don't think we're trying to be coy. It *is* convincing.

But maybe, in spite of it—perhaps *because of it*—you still have a pathetic, hopeless sort of desire to escape somehow from the necessity of lighting cigarette or cigar or pipe at regular and frequent intervals.

If you have that desire—and that's all you have to have—read on.

The guarantee doesn't end with this chapter. It applies to the whole book. Read it through and see what happens at the end. And remember that we said if you *want* to give up smoking, and you put the precepts we give you *into practice*, you *will* give it up.

Permanently.

No drugs—no tricks—nothing up the sleeve. *You will give it up!*

Want to go just a little farther?

3

The case against smoking

OF COURSE, there are always two sides to every question.

While the case in favor of smoking is almost overwhelming, there are some things to be said against it. Some few are rather important; some are seemingly minor.

But to be perfectly fair and honest before taking the book back—since you've gone this far—let's look at the other side of the picture.

Take the matter of expense, which we touched on a moment ago. Smoking was once a really inexpensive luxury; you could drop a quarter or half a dollar on the counter of a cigar store and come away with the day's supply of nicotine. Even if you were a cigar smoker, you didn't need to pay much more. Today, depending on local taxes and which of the myriad combinations of "regulars," mentholated, filtered, king size, or "hundreds" (100 millimeters long) you smoke, prices have almost doubled. In round numbers the U.S. is spending about $9 billion—not million—a year on cigarettes; more, when you include cigars and pipe tobacco.

The man who smokes two packs a day spends from perhaps $1.20 to $1.60 a day on tobacco and possibly considerably more. Taking the lowest figure, this smoker spends $10.40 a week, or $41.60 a month, or $540.80 a year to smoke. To the truly prosperous, that is not too deep a bite in the income.

Actually, that expenditure is only the beginning.

The smoker must also have a light, and this can come from a simple kitchen match or from a jeweled lighter that costs $250 or $500. Usually it comes from a less expensive lighter, which adds $2 or perhaps $5 to the citizen's smoking bill. The lighter, however, must also have fuel and an occasional new wick and flints. And lighters have a way of getting broken or lost and requiring repairs or replacement.

There are also cigarette and cigar cases.

These can cost quite a bit, too. So can pipes. Bulk considered, the pipe smoker can buy his tobacco a little cheaper than the cigarette smoker, but if he is fastidious he may also pay as much as $5 to $10 a pound for his special pipe tobacco. The cigar smoker, of course, has an especially wide range of extravagance. The national need for a good five-cent cigar is an old vaudeville joke rather than a practicality; most of them cost 10 to 15 cents each, and 50- and 75-cent luxury cigars are not uncommon. A *really* fine cigar, individually packaged, can cost $1.00 and more.

Many a businessman in only medium circumstances smokes ten 15- or 25-cent cigars a day. Even if he buys the former, that's $10.50 a week—or $546 a year. If he buys the 25-cent brand and offers one occasionally to friends or business acquaintances, he can easily pay out $1,000 a year—maybe a tenth of his annual income, literally going up in smoke.

The smoker needs other impedimenta, too: ashtrays, cigarette boxes, humidors, pipe racks, tobacco pouches, pipe cleaners and scrapers, cigarette holders, and often filters for them. And these can come high.

When you give up smoking, you give up these expenses. You may still keep cigarettes or cigars and an ashtray on your desk for visitors, and you will keep them in your home. But a lot of all these gadgets you will permanently dispense with, and you won't need to buy more.

There are certain other expenses you also eliminate from your life when you stop smoking. You will no longer ruin your best dresses or suits with burns from falling embers, and your furniture and rugs will be far safer from burn scars.

You yourself will be safer, too. You know that many fires are started by smoking in bed, or by forgetting cigarettes, or by carelessly thrown matches that were used to light tobacco. But do you know how many? The insurance underwriters say that virtually a third of all U.S. fires are caused by smoking.

Whether you ever have a fire or not, you help pay for those fires in the annual insurance rates. When you stop smoking, you are helping—microscopically, perhaps, but helping—to reduce insurance rates, since you are removing by one the number of unintentional arsonists in the country. When enough people stop smoking, fire losses will drop appreciably. So will insurance costs.

There are certain physical advantages, also, which should be taken into account in any fair appraisal.

How to **Stop Smoking**

When you give up smoking—

You'll very likely lose that little heart flutter which has been worrying you or perhaps really scaring you occasionally.

On the first night after you have stopped you will sleep better than you have in months—more soundly and more continuously.

In winter you will probably have far fewer colds, or perhaps none at all for the first time in years. Your "sinus trouble" may suddenly lessen and possibly disappear altogether.

The dyspepsia or heartburn after meals from which you may suffer is very likely to vanish —so suddenly that it will be hard to remember what it was like to have had it. (The idea that smoking is good for the digestion is romantic twaddle.)

If you have occasional hangovers from too much pleasure or business drinking at night, you will find them far less enervating and uncomfortable if you don't add smoking to the strain that drinking puts on your body. You'll be less inclined to headaches and nausea the next day.

If you are accustomed to smoking thirty cigarettes a day, you will add half an hour to every day of your life. We are not here arguing that smoking shortens your life. The point is simply that—believe it or not—smoking a single cigarette takes a trifle over one minute. That doesn't mean the time it takes to smoke the cigarette from beginning to end; while you smoke you can be, and usually are, doing other things. Nor does it include the time you may spend hunting for your pack of cigarettes (or pipe, or cigar), or for a light, or an ashtray, and so on.

It means simply the time taken to fumble one cigarette out of the package, light a match or lighter (assuming you have them on your person), and put down the cigarette two or three times and pick it up again for a puff or two during the course of smoking it. If you think we are kidding, get out your watch and time yourself on a single smoke—from the second you first reach for your cigarettes through the time it takes to light one and then put it down several times and pick it up again, and then the final snuffing out. If you are smoking out of doors and you keep the cigarette in your mouth constantly, the time is a little less, of course. Even so, you will be surprised how much of your time smoking takes up.

Does all this begin to sound interesting? Attractive? It is only the beginning.

If you think that any of it is an exaggeration, ask any heavy smoker who has stopped whether or not it is true. You don't realize it, but one of your troubles is that you have smoked so long you don't know how nice it is not to *have* to smoke.

When you give up smoking—

Your teeth will look cleaner because they *are* cleaner, and they will not require a dentist's cleaning so often.

The yellow stain on your fingers will disappear in a few days or a week.

When you get up in the morning, your mouth will not taste like the traditional inside of a motorman's glove.

You won't find your throat clogged with phlegm, and you won't find it necessary to cough or clear your throat so often, either.

Your food will taste much better. You may even find yourself becoming something of a gourmet, sensitive to the subtlest flavors, because you are no longer flooding your taste buds with some eight hundred mouthfuls of harsh smoke a day—more than many a professional fire fighter inhales in a year.

You will begin to *smell* the world around you. Remember your nose? If you're a real smoker you don't, although you may think you do. When you walk into a garden, you *smell* as well as *see* flowers; coming home at night, your nose can tell you what's for dinner before you ask; sipping an after-dinner brandy can make you understand why the French go into ecstasy over a fine cognac.

(Giving up smoking, you see, isn't all asceticism and self-denial; there are some compensations. In fact, hard as it is to believe at this stage, there are so many that when you give yourself a chance to truly appreciate them, you will never want to go back to the self-poisoning of nicotine.)

When you give up smoking—

Your nose and throat and lungs will not be continuously permeated with smoke and smoke's residue: soot.

You won't be getting ashes all over your papers or vest, or on the tablecloth or desk.

You will actually feel far less nervous. That's hard to believe—and during the first days of non-smoking you will be nervous. But it doesn't last too long, and it soon starts gradually to diminish. When you are over it, you will be surprised what sudden shocks and excitements you can meet and live through without reaching automatically for a cigarette.

You'll be calmer, more poised, and you may well find that it seems there are more hours in the day. It isn't merely that you are not wasting time lighting cigarettes, or that you are so miserable from not smoking that the time drags. Not that at all. You get over that misery

41

sooner than you think. But when you stop slowing down your body and cutting your energy with tobacco, you will find that you have so much more energy, and feel so much better adjusted, that there seems to be more time to do things and to get them done.

That sounds wildly utopian. But a lot of people know from experience that it is true.

A word of caution here. It is generally understood that when an accustomed smoker stops smoking, he or she gains weight. If you are of normal weight or underweight, there is nothing to worry about. If you have trouble with your waistline, however, remember this: when you stop smoking you will probably gain. Don't worry about it—face it! Actually you will gain not more than a few pounds. For when you stop smoking you will have a great increase in energy, and that energy you will use up—you can hardly prevent yourself from using it up! And in so doing you will burn away a lot of the weight that you put on.

More important, as we shall see in Chapter 6, during the first critical period when you really *stop* smoking—completely and permanently—there are certain rules that you will follow religiously. And so you will indulge yourself in other things, even to the extent of putting on a few pounds *temporarily*. When you have conquered the habit that has kept you in its thrall and upset your normal health for years, then will be time enough to take care of secondary matters like losing three or five pounds of excess weight.

Above all, when you stop smoking, you free yourself at last from the deadly compulsion of providing yourself with the tobacco you can't do without. You will not have to pat your pockets to make sure you have tobacco and light every time you depart for a walk or visit.

You won't have to make trips early or late to the corner drugstore for a package of cigarettes because you were so careless as to pass a tobacco stand earlier without making your daily obeisance to it.

You won't have to be bothered with carrying matches, or bumming them.

You will not have to be continually asking for an ashtray, or emptying ashtrays.

You will not interrupt movies by having to go out for a smoke, as some smokers do.

Your pockets or purse will not be continually full of loose tobacco grains; your clothes will not be bulged by pipe or pouch, cigarette pack or cigar case.

In brief, you will free your life of a burden the onerousness of which you will never have realized until you are free of it. The moment when you first walk past a tobacco shop and realize that there is no need for you to visit it is a strange and wonderful experience.

But all these things, pleasant as they may seem, are less than half of the whole. They are only extra dividends.

There are stronger reasons why you should give up smoking. Let's take a look at them— for you will find them published in very few places.

4

Why you really smoke

AS WE'VE seen, millions of people set fire to tobacco and then inhale it down to the last inch, scores of times each day. Why? Why all this expense, bother, half-admitted slavery, and personal discomfort in the form of coughs, lack of sleep, throat irritation, and the like? Few smokers know why they do it. Their explanation usually is, "I like it." Or, "Habit, I guess." Or, "Well, I've done it for years, and it doesn't do any harm."

Actually, why do people smoke? Why has smoking seized so strongly on so large a proportion of the population?

People *begin* to smoke for what might appear to be a great variety of reasons, but usually these boil down to one: social prestige. Most youngsters essay smoking at a fairly early age, in naïve, juvenile emulation of their parents, older brothers and sisters, or other heroes. Smoking is an adult trait, and children regard it with the same admiration they regard long pants or long dresses.

Also, it is usually forbidden, and that makes it doubly attractive to children (and to adults, especially women, if a despotic member of the family or the community establishes that "no decent woman smokes"). Smoking thus acquires a value completely disconnected from what is inherent in it: it is like stolen apples or making faces behind the teacher's back. It is something racy and naughty, and therefore daring, and therefore attractive. To women, especially, it presents an opportunity to prove they are sophisticated or smart, that is, women of the world. This is less operative for men since the strictures against men's smoking are far weaker.

Still, take notice of even the average man who does not smoke. Offer him a cigar or cigarette and he will refuse rather diffidently, almost apologetically, as though he is afraid you will think him a sissy. Or else he exhibits the loud aggression born of defensiveness— that is, he, too, is afraid you will think there's something wrong with him. Such is the social pressure today to be a smoker, a regular guy. And as one progresses from adolescence to adulthood, the pressure increases.

However and whenever one happens to start smoking—on a childish dare, or because the other girls in the high-school sorority do, or because one has become a college man and is virtually obligated to smoke a pipe—a person *continues* to smoke for quite another reason. What started as a childish prank or adolescent (or adult) desire to do as others do, ends by becoming a habit almost inexorably fixed on the victim.

The reason—without sounding alarmist or trying to impress you with big words—is that tobacco smoke contains not only nicotine, a poison somewhat similar to curare, but carbon monoxide, small amounts of hydrocyanic acid, pyridine, and various phenols and aldehydes. When you smoke, these are absorbed into your lungs and mouth, and then various things begin happening inside you. Your nervous system is momentarily stimulated. You start to salivate. Your blood pressure goes up. Your pulse rate increases. Tremors often appear in your hands and arms, and your extremities usually show a drop in bodily temperature. You notice none of these things, of course, if

47

you are an habitual smoker, although they are plainly detectable in the laboratory.

But what is most important of all is this: due to what you inhale (you *always* inhale tobacco smoke, regardless of whether you consciously "inhale" or think you immediately exhale it), plus the resultant irritation from these harsh fumes, plus the deeper breathing that naturally accompanies smoking, your blood vessels undergo a constriction. The effect on them is like damming up a stream or putting a flowing garden hose in a vise and tightening the vise a few turns.

It "slows you down."

That is, after the momentary stimulation, it depresses, for a far longer period, both the sympathetic and the central nervous system of the human body, as well as the endings of the motor nerves which activate the voluntary muscles.

What does that mean in your everyday life?

It means that when you smoke, you are artificially slowing down your body's normal activities. It's like closing the damper on a furnace, or putting the brakes on a moving automobile, or tying weights on the shoes of a distance runner.

Supposing you are suddenly confronted with an emergency, especially an emotional or psychological emergency—which incidentally is the only kind of emergency most of us meet in modern life. Your body still reacts as though it were a physical emergency—as though a bull were chasing you across a field, or a man had stuck a gun in your back, or someone had just announced he was going to pop you on the chin. The body gears itself for major activity; adrenalin is pumped into your blood stream, your muscles tense, you breathe faster, some people's ears even perk up like a dog's—the whole body strips for action like the crew of a battleship going into an attack. All of which means that you get edgy, jittery—"nervous."

Tobacco smoke retards these natural processes by constricting your arteries, slowing down the blood circulation, and thus "calming you down." So you find a smoke is "good for your nerves." Have you a critical college examination to study for? Or had a few words with an impolite waiter? Or faced playing a piano solo before a big audience? A cigarette helps.

Sure it does. It depresses these bodily activities that have been stirred to emergency pitch and have no proper physical outlet. And if that's as far as it went there would be no occasion for your worrying about smoking—or for reading this book.

For if you smoked a cigarette or cigar or pipe only at times of really critical emotional stress and strain, it would, all in all, probably be a good thing for you. But you don't. Smoking goes much farther than that. Certainly thirty to fifty genuine emergencies don't arise each day. Yet that's the number of times you light up, if you are a heavy or moderately heavy smoker.

What has happened is that you have let yourself get into a habit. Your physique has come to expect feeling this depressant, "soothing" effect every so often. If it doesn't get it, you begin consciously to *want* a cigarette or cigar.

At first you may smoke for small and often almost unconscious reasons—perhaps merely because of the vague discomfort occasioned by eating a heavy meal. But presently, when your body becomes habituated to tobacco, you *want* a smoke fairly regularly. It's not that you really enjoy it. It's that you are unhappy—more and more acutely unhappy, as the years of habit fix themselves on you—if you *don't* have it.

If you smoke a pack and a half of cigarettes a day, you smoke one cigarette every thirty-two minutes, on the average (assuming you sleep eight hours a night). If you are a two-pack smoker, it's one cigarette every twenty-four minutes. That many crises don't arise every day! You don't that often need tobacco's reassurance that you are grown up or sophisticated! And you certainly don't need such frequent "pleasures" to make life bearable. You need cigarettes simply because your body has become habituated to want them.

We mentioned pleasures. Only the naïve say or think that they smoke for pleasure. Usually the veteran smoker is more bitterly honest.

Burning tobacco is not greatly different from other burning vegetation—wood, leaves, or weeds. And while the scent of wood smoke is a very pleasant thing when caught at a little distance on a winter's day walk, and the incense of burning leaves is a fragrant concomitant of autumn, neither of them is especially enjoyable when you stick your head right into them and inhale deeply. But that's what you do with tobacco.

Medically speaking, tobacco is not habit-forming—that is, it does not worm its way into your physique and psyche, as opium or cocaine do. But it *is* habit-forming in the same way that three meals a day, or eight hours' sleep, or wearing clothes, are habit-forming. Try going without any of them for a while and see how comfortable you are.

51

But how comfortable are you *with* tobacco? Smoke a cigarette. Does it really satisfy you—in the way that a big steak does when you're hungry, or a warm coat when you're cold? You know better. Of course it doesn't. Light it, smoke it, taste its harsh bitterness, put it out. Even as you do, you know that you'll soon *want* another and be lighting it. Not that you enjoy it. You simply want it.

What do you enjoy? If it were possible by some magic trick for you to go without cigarettes for the next twenty-four or forty-eight hours, and then light one, you would find out how really unpleasant and noxious tobacco smoke is. Two deep inhalations, and you would find your head swimming, your brain giddy, your legs and arms shaky. You might even feel faint and have to sit down. If you think that is an exaggeration, try it. Or think back to the time many, many years ago when you smoked your first cigarette. Divorced from all the glamour and excitement of your first smoke, how did it *taste?* Gaseous, strong, biting, wasn't it?

Yet this is the "pleasant, fragrant anodyne" that you take into your system not once but thirty to sixty times a day. The only reason you are able to do it is because the human mechanism is a marvelously adjustable piece of machinery which can get used to living amid coal dust, or 110-degree heat, or doing the work of a truck horse. You can get used to all these things. But don't think any of them are good for you, or are pleasant, or help you live longer.

No, smoking is not pleasant until you inure your body to it so that it puts up with tobacco's effects—the harsh taste, the hot dryness, the mouth bite—for the sake of its mild narcotic effect. It is not pleasant until you've read or listened to thousands of advertisements that tell you how fragrant and soothing and mellow and mild and aromatic and tasty and God-knows-what-else tobacco smoke is. After that you're not smoking tobacco. You are smoking habit, and advertising copy.

Unlike the American Medical Association, which has occasionally cracked down on the claims made by the cigarette companies, or the Fair Trade Commission, which has accused some of them of "misleading" advertising, we have no quarrel with the tobacco companies. They are competitive business organizations doing their best to sell their product. To do that, they employ the best advertising men they can get (and the best artists, and prettiest girls, and most influential "endorsers," whether or not they happen to

53

smoke at all, much less that particular brand). But all these are merely aggressive business tactics. The fault is less with the tobacco companies than with the customers who are foolish enough to use their product to excess. Whom would you blame if everyone started eating corn flakes to excess, to the point where they could not enjoy corn flakes, and were endangering their health? The corn-flakes makers or their customers?

Let's leave the manufacturers out of this and not start feeling sorry for ourselves as victims of the "tobacco interests." But, to be perfectly fair all around, let's also bear this in mind: in the last twenty years this country has come to realize there is an ailment known as alcoholism. More and more cities and states are opening clinics and taking other measures to help the alcoholic redeem himself. And rightly so, surely. But did you ever hear of a permanent clinic for a nicotinic—of whom there are probably ten for every helpless drinker? The nicotinic doesn't go to pot as theatrically as does the alcoholic, but he has something of the same problem. He's the victim of a desire which looks bigger than he is, which he has sworn off time and again, and which he cannot put an end to. That's how this book happened to be written.

The author smoked heavily for years. One night at home he ran out of cigarettes—through carelessness. And through laziness he did not rush out and buy some. Next morning, driving to the office, he realized that for the first time in many, many years, he had gone some fourteen hours without smoking. It was a novel and challenging situation. How long would it last? Instead of stopping at the first smoke shop, he drove to the office—where cigarettes were near at hand.

But out of a kind of adventurous feeling of experiment he tried to see how long he could go without smoking. Until noon? After lunch? Until evening? He never felt that it would last more than a day.

It lasted eighteen months—and it was a tremendously enlightening personal experience. How he started smoking again is another story which will presently be taken up. And so will the story of his finally swearing off for good.

The point is that, having given up smoking and being surrounded, among friends and business associates, by heavy smokers, he discovered that there was a lot of interest on the part of everyone in giving up smoking. How you did it and how you kept it up. And why the dickens you ever started smoking in the first place.

The author began experimenting with himself as subject, and also by questioning others who had given up smoking or had tried to. It became a sort of hobby asking people: Why do you smoke, what do you get out of it, have you tried to stop, and do you want to stop? And it was quickly found that smoking was something everyone thought about and liked to talk about.

And felt very helpless about.

Hence this book. For when he wants to stop smoking, the smoker has few effective sympathizers. His smoking friends tell him it's impossible or just too tough. His non-smoking friends tell him, with some superiority, that they cannot understand how anyone smokes; period.

So he is forced into a rebellious, ashamed, or frustrated frame of mind in which he upbraids himself for his lack of "will power" (we'll explode that one shortly) and, if he thinks about it long enough, works himself into such a state that he gets "nervous" and then has to light a cigarette to quiet his nerves.

Or else, in a gesture of wild desperation, he throws cigarettes, pipes, cigars, or whatever out the window, announces he has given up smoking—and sticks to it for two hours or two days. Then, sheepishly, he lights up.

And that is one small example of the real inescapable reason why you should give up smoking. Not merely because of the expense, although stopping can help your budget. Not merely because of your health, although the main bulk of medicine's conflicting evidence indicates that smoking and many bodily difficulties are closely associated. Not because it's "immoral" or "unclean," or because some bluenoses regard smoking as a vicious vice and non-smoking as a special kind of virtue.

You should give up smoking because, up to now, you have secretly felt that it has you licked—and maybe it has. As we've said, it isn't that you really enjoy smoking; it is just that you are unhappy without it. It is a habit which you have permitted to become so much a part of you that you are its slave, its unwilling devotee who regularly must pay tribute out of your energy and sleep, well-being and happiness.

To support tobacco's hold on you, you have given up time and money and comfort, and you know, and for a long time have known, that there is something wrong in that. It has made you feel foolish, weak, and guilty—not the Puritan meaning of guilt which holds that all pleasure is bad, but the kind of guilt which any person of normal intelligence and sensibility experiences in the face of the knowledge that he has let himself drift into a useless and annoying habit which he cannot break.

Enough of this; let's go to work. This book is guaranteed, remember, to enable you to give up smoking permanently, if you follow its instructions. Maybe we've told you enough to assure you that we know what we're talking about. That we know what tobacco tastes like, and how it feels, and why a smoker smokes, even when his mouth is sore from smoking, or his head aches from it, or a cold deadens him to everything except tobacco's dulling effect.

In the next chapter we're going to tell you about the preliminary preparations—how you get ready to start. Don't get scared. You're not going to stop smoking yet. We're just going to tell you about the first steps to take, if and when you decide to.

So meanwhile—feel nervous?—by all means light up and enjoy yourself.

5

The preliminaries

WHILE giving up smoking is any-thing but easy, its difficulties can and have been exaggerated, especially by the smoker himself, as he ponders his discouraging plight.

Nevertheless, although things are not as bad as he thinks, they are bad enough so that he would do well to employ every really useful, practical device, every psychological trick that he can, to help in the forthcoming bat-tle.

These are not to be confused with the time-worn and usually unsuccessful methods which most heavy smokers have tried at one time or another. Let's consider these last for just a moment.

The simplest and possibly most futile, for example, is the *sudden break*, made entirely on angry impulse. You suddenly get fed up with smoking—usually on a morning after a late night when you have smoked your mouth into a state of tingling, bitter rawness. Remorseful and disgusted, you suddenly announce that you are through with smoking. That lasts about as long as the raw feeling in your mouth or throat. Then the old yearning returns and you light a cigarette, and it doesn't taste so good, but it doesn't taste so bad either, and you acknowledge shamefacedly that you've lost another battle.

The *reduction* or *ration method* is very nearly as futile. In this case you resolve to smoke only a certain number of cigarettes a day—a pack or maybe only a dozen. Or you decide to smoke twenty cigarettes today, but only nineteen tomorrow, and eighteen on the day after that, and so on until you are down to five a day—or maybe none at all. You tell yourself that whichever method you choose, it will make you enjoy each smoke more (which is true, if you can really do it), because a lot of your smoking is automatic. You frequently smoke four or five cigarettes in succession without being aware of it until you see the telltale butts in your ashtray.

The trouble with this method is that it is almost more trouble than smoking is; you find yourself looking at the clock (time for another?), or counting the cigarettes in your pack (how many left for today?), or worrying whether you should smoke now or save one for after lunch. And so on.

This self-disciplining may last for a day or several days, and then either you tire of all the bookkeeping, or else some emergency comes along and knocks your resolution into a cocked hat. You tell yourself that when the emergency is over, you will get back on schedule. But you never do.

The *acute-discomfort method* is probably the least popular way of "giving up smoking." You make a bet with someone for a sizable sum, which it would be painful to lose, that you can stop smoking for a month or for three months. Or you purposely go around without cigarettes and make yourself borrow from friends when you want a smoke, depending on your own self-respect to curtail your borrowing and therefore your smoking.

The trouble with this one is that you are really shifting the burden of responsibility from yourself to someone else, when actually no one but yourself can help you. True, if you have made the bet big enough to be painful,

you may go on to win it. But the instant you
have, you will want, and probably light, a cigarette. For you have not really given up
smoking; you merely stopped for financial reasons. And, again, you presently come to be so
ashamed of your borrowing that in self-defense
you tell yourself you have to buy some cigarettes of your own. You do. And so it goes.

A personal campaign to get rid of the smoking habit is most likely to succeed and be least
painful if you go about it intelligently—in-
formed in advance of what you may expect,
with full knowledge of what you are giving up,
and of the means of help that are at your dis-
posal. That is the purpose of this and the next
chapter. In this one we will discuss the simple
preliminary steps to take. In the next, you will
learn of the various tricks and aids which will
start you on your way and then help to keep
you on it.

Concerning the preliminaries:

1. FORGET WILL POWER!

Will power is one of the great modern buga-
boos. To most people, it suggests a man who
can somehow conquer anything: he grits his
teeth, frowns intently, flexes his muscles, and

somehow forces himself through to success in whatever he has set himself to do, whether it be climbing a mountain, earning a million dollars, or giving up smoking. Conversely, it suggests that if you try to do these things and can't, you have weak will power or none at all and are a spineless sissy. That is baloney.

Will power is simply a set of habits, that is, a well-grooved neural pattern which has been established by your wants, or likes and dislikes. In general, you do what you do because it is what you want to do. A man scales a difficult mountain because he likes mountain climbing, or loves acclaim, or is a natural explorer. Another man builds a million-dollar fortune because to him a million dollars is very nearly the most important thing in the world, and perhaps is the most important.

An elevator boy, weary of the tiresome ups and downs of his job, day in, day out, may tell a friend around the pool room that he wants a million dollars more than anything in the world. And he thinks he does. If he really wanted it, he would be saving his money and studying how to invest it so as to bring him more, not hanging around pool rooms. Eventually he might wind up with a million. Or he might not, but he would get a part of it— and be very happy in the process.

If he is a pool-room lounger at heart and tries to drive himself—by will power—to save, study finance and business, he may well end up in a nervous breakdown. So might a man who, fearing heights or lonely rugged terrain, drove himself to climb mountains.

That is why, at the start, we guaranteed that *if you really want to give up smoking you can*, and with this book's help, *you will*. All you need is the desire and the willingness to follow these instructions.

Forget about your will power or lack of it—you don't need it.

As a matter of fact, any psychologist will tell you there is no such thing.

2. START THINKING ABOUT IT

It ought to encourage you to know that, even though you don't realize it, you have already taken one big step toward giving up smoking. For you have already read this far, which means that, for that long at least, you have been *thinking* about giving it up.

And that is an important rule if you want to stop smoking: think about giving it up.

Think of it coolly and calmly, without fear or hopelessness. Many others have done it.

You can, too. Consider the whole idea objectively a little while.

If you are not smoking right at this very minute, maybe it would be a good idea to take out cigarette or pipe and light them up. Analyze what you do and what you taste and smell. Drag the smoke into your lungs slowly and slowly exhale it. Just how good is it, really? Does it have the fragrance and goodness and "satisfaction" the copy writers claim?

Think for a moment of how much you get out of it, of how pleasurable it really is—aside from the negative pleasure of easing an otherwise painful habit.

Then think of what it would be like not ever to *have* to smoke.

Think about it just a moment as you go to bed at night, and refer to it once or twice during the day. Don't try to make even a tentative resolution! Except perhaps one: One of these days, when I feel like it, maybe I'll *try* going without smoking and see what happens. Don't grit your teeth or frown or clench your jaw or start waving your arms. Just consider the possibility of stopping for a while as an experiment, as a little change of pace in the regular routine of your existence.

That is, *think* about it. That's all.

3. MAKE A LIST

The third preliminary is: Now or within the next few days—preferably now!—make a list of all the things you don't like about smoking. Just jot them down and number them—a single word is enough to describe each thing you don't like. But be sure you *do it*—don't postpone it indefinitely.

Maybe you won't think of all the things at once. Going over some of the points we made in Chapter 3 might help. But the chances are that as you go on smoking during the next few days other things will occur to you. Add them to your list—on a card, perhaps, carried in wallet or purse.

Again, that's all—just make a list. And keep it. You'll use it later.

4. DON'T BE AFRAID

As we've said earlier, it has become a national superstition that a veteran smoker can't stop. But superstition is just what that is. If you found yourself feeling unwell and went to a doctor, and he told you that either you must stop smoking or else prepare for an early death—

you would stop smoking right away. Why wait for such a possibility, remote as it may be?

You can stop now, and the only thing you have to fear is fear. Giving up smoking entails a marked change in your whole physique, but that is nothing to drive you skulking into a corner. It will be a pleasant change. The depressant effect smoking has exerted on your body for years suddenly ends when you stop. You will find yourself feeling "jittery" for that reason. You will very possibly be more emotional, laughing longer at more trivial things and, for a while, tenser, jumping higher at smaller noises. That will be uncomfortable.

But you will also find yourself bursting with energy and impatient to get things done. That is not a bad feeling, by the way, although at first it is sometimes disconcerting. You see, it has been years since your body, which is really a delicate and powerful machine, has had a chance to deliver to you all the things of which it is capable. You have kept it in the strait jacket of the tobacco habit. When it starts suddenly to get back to normal, the unfamiliar effect is almost overwhelming.

So for a while you will feel nervous and jumpy and odd. But, as we've seen, there are compensations, such as not having to bother with tobacco's impedimenta, the adventurous feeling of freedom and of being your own boss, the luxuries of sleeping better and feeling better. These, too, begin to take effect as soon as you stop.

They help. They won't outweigh the discomfort—at first, anyway. That's going to be a wrench, and let's not kid ourselves. But if you are really, deeply afraid of that, it's probably a good thing. For you can then be sure it is not going to be as bad as you think it is. Bad it will be. But not so bad that you can't take it.

That is the thing *not* to be afraid of! A healthy respect for the enemy is always wholesome and helpful. And in this case you are up against a sufficiently tough enemy so that you must prepare yourself for a real fight.

Just don't handicap yourself by being so abjectly fearful that you go into the fight more than half convinced you can't win. To think that is just plain silly.

5. WATCH AND WAIT

The last preliminary is simple but important, for it governs your selection of the best time for your own personal D-Day—or S- (for Stop) Day. Remember, during the next few days or weeks you are going to *think* about giving up smoking. As you do, you'll begin

to realize that the idea is not completely ter-
rifying or impossible. And you will also, remember, begin to think of just *trying* it at
some time or other.

The time to try it is not when you are leav-
ing on an important business trip or preparing
to give a big dinner or bridge party, or when
you are facing some personal emergency.

Watch and wait until some time when your
life is on a fairly even keel—no especially
difficult times in prospect for the next few
days anyway. Don't postpone it too long, of
course, or you will lose the momentum you
are gradually building up.

But some morning—maybe on a weekend
—you will wake up feeling especially good.
You will have had a good night's sleep, you
feel fit for anything, and the sun is shining
sweetly.

And the idea of stopping smoking will pop
into your head. Somehow it will not seem
quite so impossible as it might at other times.
And it will occur to you that maybe this is the
day—S-Day!

Then and there—on the spur of the moment!—tell yourself you are through smoking.

You have fulfilled all the preliminaries first,
remember. You have not been badgering yourself about your lack of "will power." You've

been thinking about stopping, at odd moments for some days. You've made your list of all the things you don't like about it. You've begun to realize that you've nothing to be afraid of.

Now, quietly and firmly decide you're through with it! This is the moment, intelligently selected and properly prepared for, when you can start off with the running start of feeling *good!*

Why foul up a swell morning with the noxious fumes of burning nicotine and pyridine and aldehydes? Why shoulder for another day the burden you've been carrying for years—of your own stupid volition? Why walk back into your jail cell, a voluntary prisoner for another day, when the door to the prison stands wide open?

This is it!

After thinking about it for years, after sporadic and badly planned, ignorant efforts to rid yourself of smoking—this is the time you do it!

It's going to be tough at first, but you are prepared for that.

And, to help you much more, the next two chapters are devoted to balanced, tested, sound advice and tips on how to keep going.

From S-Day morning on, when someone offers you a cigarette, you can refuse and say, "Thanks, I don't smoke."

And when you do, *you* won't say it apologetically. For unlike the person who never started, you have smoked and have quit. And that's something to be proud of.

6

The weapons at your disposal;
or, you're better off than you think

MARK TWAIN is reported to be the author of a superbly cynical remark about giving up smoking. "It is easy to give up smoking," he said. "I have done it thousands of times."

The author might make somewhat the same claim, although for a different reason. We have not given up smoking thousands of times, but we have done it a number of times, with various purposes in mind. After giving it up for eighteen months, for example, we started smoking again because of. nervous tension caused by business pressure.

But, having once experienced a good long term of the pleasures of non-smoking—sleeping better, feeling healthier, being more alert, vigorous, and relaxed—we could never again completely forget it and return as before to the old ways. So presently we gave it up again, for approximately a year. And again presently started to smoke once more because of certain disturbing happenings.

It was at this point that we began considering writing this book.

For, having twice given up smoking for extended periods, we were beginning to know the problem. Like a pioneer who twice made the long trek from Missouri to the West Coast during the days of the wagon trains, we began to feel like a veteran in comparison with those who had never made the trip yet wanted to. That was when we began to experiment purposefully with smoking and non-smoking, and to read on the subject and think about it.

More than once we stopped smoking and then started again, to analyze how we felt and what it did to and for us. Sometimes in the middle of a period of abstention we deliberately smoked one cigarette, inhaling it deeply, "enjoying" it to the fullest possible extent. (That is a wonderfully illuminating experience, by the way, and it is a pity that the average heavy smoker cannot, for reasons we will explain farther on, safely experience it; at any

rate, not for the first several years of abstention.) For that one cigarette tasted perfectly
terrible. A smoke never tastes good until you
have thoroughly soaked your system, your
nasal passages, and your taste buds with the
nicotine of dozens of cigarettes or cigars.

This is an honest book, and so it is necessary to report that almost every time we re-
turned to tobacco after a period of self-imposed
abstention, there was a period, after the initial
readjustment to its noxious fumes and tongue-
irritating "fragrance" was past, that it seemed
good and soothing and pleasant to be smoking again.

But now there was a difference. After many
years of smoking, of dependence on tobacco
and of becoming so accustomed to the incon-
veniences it causes that we were almost un-
aware of them, we now had a norm by which
to judge and appraise these things. That is,
lurking in the back of our mind, even when
cigarette or pipe tasted best, was the knowledge that this was an acquired taste and that
acquiring it and enjoying it cost us a lot of
other things which actually were pleasanter.
We had the memory of how we felt during the
non-smoking periods and, once a person who
has smoked for years experiences that, he
never forgets it.

And never secretly stops desiring to return to abstention. There is nothing moral or "upright" about it in the ordinary sense. It is simply an intelligent weighing of two pleasures, smoking and not smoking, and choosing the one which yields the greatest ultimate satisfaction.

And so, quite simply, we gave up smoking for good and decided to put what we had learned about it in a book, so that other people might benefit from it, too. And might learn that there *is* a way out—so sure and so practical that we have ventured to make a guarantee about it, based only on the condition that you really desire to stop smoking and put these precepts into practice.

During the months and years that we experimented with smoking, we became interested in the phase of psychology dealing with habit formation and re-formation. For someone who wants to break himself of a habit which seems to have him badly licked, that is very heartening reading.

For the professional psychologist knows a lot more about you than you may suppose, and he can give you advice and suggestions that are as practical and helpful as the advice of a good golf pro who has taught thousands of average golfers suffering from the faults and weaknesses that you possess.

This chapter represents a summary of that sort of knowledge, and we'd like to suggest that you read it carefully and thoughtfully and return to it, and to the next chapter also, several times before you launch on your own campaign to stop smoking. In one sense, it is the very heart of the book, and for that reason we have furnished it with subtitles which are short and easy to memorize. If you will take the trouble to learn them, you will acquire a few bits of knowledge that will apply not only to the period of your giving up smoking but to many other habits, all your life.

Before we begin them, there is one very important point we learned the hard way, and which we'd like to emphasize at the start. At the moment you give up smoking, whenever that may be (and it's going to come sooner or later), make it a rule to:

> BABY YOURSELF IN EVERY-
> THING ELSE

Don't try to give up smoking and, if you drink, drinking at the same time. Or don't go on a diet simultaneously, either. If you like candy, don't give that up; and if you are the sort of

76

person who's long been threatening to start a program of daily workouts, or do exercises to reduce, or anything of that sort—don't start such a regimen until you are at least a couple of weeks on your non-smoking way. A lot of us are inclined to launch sudden, widely ambitious programs of self-improvement which are actually complete revolutions in our everyday lives. Such programs usually defeat their own purpose; we try to do more than we can reasonably expect of ourselves. The sensible plan is to do one thing at a time and do it well.

So, when you decide to give up smoking, baby yourself in everything else. The one thing you are going to do is to give up a habit which has held you a prisoner for many years, and if you succeed in that, you will have done enough for yourself for a while.

Don't increase the difficulties of it by simultaneously adding others.

On the contrary, instead of giving up fattening or particularly delicious foods, in addition to depriving yourself of tobacco, eat what you want and enjoy it thoroughly. That is, indulge yourself. If you like a shrimp cocktail or a filet mignon or an eclair for dinner, and feel you shouldn't or can't afford it, go ahead and have it!

Remember, you are cutting down on expenses, among other things, when you stop smoking. So, particularly during the first critical stage of your abstention, you are entitled to some other luxuries, and, from the standpoint of pennies, you are earning them.

Again, if you like to take a drink occasionally, by all means take one when you feel like it. Or two. Let yourself go a little in this and in other things, always bearing in mind that you are entitled to this indulgence because you have earned it by giving up something else. (It is hardly necessary to say that we would be deeply chagrined, to say the least, if anyone accepted this as advice to get plastered and run his car into a tree.)

But during the first few weeks of your giving up smoking, recognize that you are trying to break a deeply embedded habit which has persisted for perhaps half of your lifetime. What is at stake is worth whatever it may cost to make it a little easier for yourself. Once you are "over the hump," there will be time to apply your newly acquired knowledge of habit making and breaking to other, less harmful ones.

In the same way, make it a habit to buy and carry mints, gum, salted nuts, or to have an occasional cup of coffee or glass of soda when you feel the desire to smoke. That is important. If you are not accustomed to such tidbits, you may think this is a little *too* self-indulgent. It isn't. You won't put a fresh stick of gum into your mouth as often as you would normally smoke a cigarette, and, even if you did, you would be better off than if you smoked. And you would spend only about a cent more than you would if you smoked, for a stick of gum costs around one cent against two cents, in round numbers. You can still buy a Coke more cheaply than a decent cigar.

So remember that whenever you stop smoking, you will buy a package of gum and a package of Life Savers or something similar, even if you don't want them at that moment. Carry them in your pocket or purse, and as you work, read, or play, pop one into your mouth when you feel the urge to indulge in a smoke. And eat or chew as much as you want.

This is far more important than you may think, so even if you never normally eat mints, chew gum, or drink soda, please arrange to do so temporarily. You should have them on hand at least during the first week, and preferably the first two weeks.

Don't worry about getting the gum or candy-eating habit! As the desire to smoke dies, so will the desire for a substitute.

How to Stop Smoking

With this basic idea in mind, let's go on to some advice by a great psychologist. William James's reputation has been overshadowed by Sigmund Freud's, but, basically a pragmatist —which means that he was chiefly interested in the practical application of what he observed and discovered—James's observations on habits and their making and breaking are of extraordinary value to us right now.

As a matter of fact, the chapter on Habit in his monumental *Psychology* has been widely reprinted and quoted. Freud became the world's most famous psychologist by exploring the subconscious and evolving theories about it; James preferred to observe himself and his fellow men and thus to evolve practical theories about behavior. The Freudians can offer you an interesting (and disputed) theory as to *why* you smoke. James can tell you how to put a stop to smoking or to any other habit.

Let's look at his advice on habits, and if we may be permitted to paraphrase him very considerably, apply it directly to the habit of tobacco smoking.

To begin with, let it be clearly understood, if it is not already, that smoking is a habit and that habits are acquired modes of behavior. For example, if you are a man, you are in the habit of wearing trousers, and if you are a woman, you are accustomed to skirts. You weren't born like that; wearing skirts or pants became a habit, ingrained by custom and usage. When custom decrees that men wear skirts (Scotch Highlanders, for example), they do it without self-consciousness. In any case, the habit is supported by a need—the need for protecting oneself from the elements, dirt, and rough surfaces.

All habits, then, are acquired and begin with a need. Smoking, as we have seen, is the result of a need for calming ourselves down. Bad habits are seldom bad in themselves; they are simply normal tendencies carried to excess. It is natural to like to lie in bed late occasionally, but do it every day and it becomes laziness. It is natural to take a narcotic prescription to ease pain, but do it every day and you become a drug addict. There's nothing wrong with an occasional cigarette to soothe your nerves, but carry it to excess and you are a tobacco addict. You have acquired a bad habit. As a matter of fact, *it* has acquired *you*.

Now your task is to *un*acquire it.

To unacquire or get rid of such habits, James formulated four great principles which we herewith apply to smoking. Think about them and remember them.

81

How to Stop Smoking

ONE: START YOURSELF OFF ON THE NEW WAY OF LIFE WITH AS MUCH MOMENTUM AS YOU CAN.

Tell your friends that you have given up smoking. Don't be smug or complacent or boastful, but by all means let people know what you are doing. When they tell you (and they will!) that it can't be done, don't get mad or act superior. Pleasantly tell them to wait and see. At some point when you are seriously tempted to smoke, the thought of all the derisive laughter you'll get for giving in may well carry you over the crisis, which is the reason you should tell others about what you are doing.

If there are certain occasions or associations which are likely to tempt you to smoke, avoid them at least for a few days. If that is impossible, brace yourself in advance for such temptations; tell yourself that such an occasion is coming, and you must be prepared to want to smoke badly yet not give in to that want.

Pick a time for stopping when you are less likely to encounter such occasions. A vacation is a fine time; so, even, is a weekend which promises to be relaxing and quiet. Then wait until the moment when you really feel ready— it will come, a day or a week or a month after you finish this book—and loudly announce to the world that you are through smoking.

SECOND: DON'T PERMIT YOURSELF TO MAKE A SINGLE EXCEPTION TO YOUR NEW RULE UNTIL THE NON-SMOKING HABIT IS FIRMLY IMPLANTED (and that will be a long time).

A habit is like many forms of animal life; if it is not fed at all, it dies relatively quickly, but it can subsist for a long time on the slightest, least nourishing kinds of foods. That is, if you occasionally let yourself have one cigarette or pipe on the ground that "just one won't hurt," you will keep alive far longer the desire to smoke. In other words, you simply will intensify and prolong your own torture.

As a matter of fact, if you give in at all, you will probably give in completely and begin smoking as heavily as ever. One drink is too many for an alcoholic, because once he starts, he cannot stop. The same is true, less dramatically perhaps, of the heavy smoker who is trying to reform. Every time you say "no" to the temptation to smoke, you are driving another nail in the coffin nails' coffin. You are making the next "no" easier to say.

Once you have stopped, don't let the desire to smoke persuade you that while this moment of temptation is tough, the next will be tougher, and the next, and the next tougher still. They won't. The tough moments come only one at a time, and they get easier as you defeat them one at a time. All you have to do is win the battle of the moment and forget about an hour from now, or a day from now, or a week from now. Defeat one temptation, and the next one won't be quite so tempting.

James's third principle is:

THIRD: ONCE YOU HAVE DETERMINED TO GIVE UP SMOKING, DO IT AT THE FIRST GOOD CHANCE WHICH OFFERS.

We've already gone into the preliminaries. The important thing is not merely to read this book and work yourself up into a fever of enthusiasm to stop smoking—but to *stop!*

If you let your hope and enthusiasm gradually die while you postpone, too long, putting your intentions into effect, you either will never actually stop smoking, or you will do it when most or all of the help you can give yourself is lost.

You must pick your time intelligently, of course, as we have seen. But when the time comes—go to work! If some of the things you have read thus far struck home, if this book has partly or completely described how you feel about smoking, about its slavery and unpleasantness and the seeming hopelessness of it, and if, while reading it, you have been occasionally stirred to believe that maybe it would be possible after all for *you* to give it up—then for heaven's sake don't let that valuable hope and desire escape from you! It is the sustenance for your whole campaign. If you let it rot and wither, like supplies in an abandoned warehouse, you will never have anything to fight with.

When the time comes, don't flinch.

Don't postpone it.

Don't weakly tell yourself, "Later."

Pick the right time, and then—do it!

FINALLY: DON'T MERELY GIVE UP SMOKING AND THEN MEEKLY, PASSIVELY, SUBMIT TO ITS TEMPORARY DISCOMFORTS. FIGHT THEM ACTIVELY BY DELIBERATELY EXPOSING YOURSELF TO SMALL TEMPTATIONS AND CONQUERING THEM.

That is, just as a fighter conditions himself for a major fight by road work and sparring, you can develop your determination by deliberate "workouts."

Don't lie down supinely, accept the "torture," and resign yourself to waiting for it to end. Meet it head on. If you are accustomed to riding in the smoker in trains, continue to do so, and look at all the people around you who are riding there by necessity and not choice, as you are doing. They can't give up smoking. You have!

Carry matches and light cigarettes or cigars for your friends.

Make it a point every day to go out of your way at least once to demonstrate how you have forsworn tobacco.

Inhale the smoke from someone else's pipe or cigarette and then remind yourself (how well you know it!) that it smells far better, caught in brief whiffs like this, than it does when it is you who are inhaling its noxious fumes deep into your lungs.

If you want to give yourself a real test and a sense of hard-won victory, go deliberately into a smoke shop, buy a pack of your favorite brand of cigarettes, open them, and smell the tobacco. Remember, it smells much more fragrant like that than when a burning coal is turning it into hot and bitter smoke.

Then give the pack to someone else.

If these tests sound too dangerously tempting, don't try them, especially during the first few days. Or try something milder to "train" and develop your growing courage. But *try something*, even if it is only watching a friend enjoy a cigarette after a meal.

That is, go out and meet the enemy halfway. Don't rest on your oars and tell yourself what a terrible ordeal this is. If you deliberately go out of your way to make it tough, it will seem far less so, and you will much sooner get over the worst of it, which usually lasts about a week.

There are some other vitally important weapons in your arsenal. But before we look at them let's summarize—and memorize—what we have learned. Remember, you are going to:

> 1. START YOUR CAMPAIGN UNDER THE MOST AUSPICIOUS CIRCUMSTANCES AND WITH ALL THE MOMENTUM YOU CAN.
>
> 2. FIGHT OFF EACH INDIVIDUAL TEMPTATION AS IT OCCURS, WITHOUT WORRYING ABOUT FUTURE ONES.
>
> 3. SEIZE THE FIRST GOOD CHANCE THAT COMES ALONG AND . . . GIVE . . . UP . . . SMOKING! DON'T TAKE IT OUT IN GOOD INTENTIONS.

4. FIGHT BACK TEMPTATION BY DELIBERATELY EXPOSING YOUR-SELF TO ONE SMALL ONE EACH DAY.

A number of years ago a Frenchman named Coué made a great name for himself in this country by coming here and preaching the doctrine of autosuggestion. Said he: Just tell yourself, "Every day in every way I am getting better and better," and you will.

This got to be something of a national joke, as you may or may not remember. But Coué's doctrine contained a hard kernel of psychological fact.

If you keep telling yourself something often enough and firmly enough, it will become a fact for you.

If you tell yourself that you are going to give up smoking—if you even *think* of giving up smoking long enough and longingly enough —you will give it up.

That isn't the end of it, of course. You have to implement your decision with other psychological weapons such as those we discuss in this chapter and in the next.

But if today—right now—you tell yourself that one of these days you are going to give up smoking, and you repeat it tomorrow, and repeat it several times the next day, sooner or later you will stop smoking. Once you have stopped, you can use the same technique to strengthen your resolution. You tell yourself, as you walk or ride to work, or get breakfast, or do the chores, that today you are not going to smoke. You are not a smoker.

If you merely tell yourself several times each day, after you have stopped, that you no longer are a smoker, or that you really don't want to smoke, it will help you a lot.

Sound silly? Maybe it does. But it isn't.

At first you may find it hard to say that convincingly to yourself. You may even feel sheepish, secretly thinking that though you have given up smoking, it can't last, and that pretty soon you will break down and start to smoke again. Never mind. Follow the rule:

START TELLING YOURSELF YOU ARE GOING TO STOP. AFTER YOU HAVE, TELL YOURSELF THAT YOU ARE NO LONGER A SMOKER AND DON'T REALLY WANT TO SMOKE.

Never mind if it is hard to believe. Say it anyway. Belief will come with experience— the experience of really not smoking.

In a book called *Release From Nervous Tension,* which is well worth your attention and is remarkably easy to read, despite its rather forbidding title, the author, Dr. David Harold Fink, includes a brief discussion of a psychological technique known as "controlled sleep."

Like many another psychological phrase, "controlled sleep" sounds grimly technical. Actually it is a very simple matter. As Dr. Fink points out, it was used by generations of American Indians to win adult status for themselves.

As an Indian boy began to grow up, at a certain time he would retreat to a secluded spot to sleep in the expectation of dreaming about an animal. This was a tribal tradition. In due time he did dream of an animal, and that became his name—Little Bear, Running Deer, Sitting Bull, or whatever he dreamt of. It never failed, because he expected to dream of an animal and wanted to.

If you want to give up smoking, you can make controlled sleep help you enormously. In fact, if you never followed any other of the rules set down here (and you should, to keep your end of the bargain), controlled sleep could get you over the hump of stopping.

What you do is simply this:

On the night of the first day that you give

up smoking, go to bed as usual and think for a moment of how today you did not smoke. Think of the various times during the day when you were tempted to, yet did not, give in. Then tell yourself, "Tomorrow I am not going to smoke. Tobacco tastes awful. Tomorrow I am not going to smoke. Tobacco tastes awful. Tomorrow I am not going to . . ."

Repeat it to yourself as you get drowsy. That isn't hard, and it isn't even hard to believe.

You got through the first day, didn't you? As you drop off to sleep, it won't be hard to believe that you can do the same thing tomorrow.

So keep telling yourself, "Tomorrow I am not going to smoke."

When you wake up in the morning, remind yourself that you are going to get through this day without smoking.

Don't clench your teeth or tense your muscles or make a big issue of it. Just—briefly —say: "This day I don't smoke."

And see what happens.

So we come to the last of our six major rules:

PRACTICE CONTROLLED SLEEP, TELLING YOURSELF EACH NIGHT BEFORE YOU GO TO BED THAT TOBACCO TASTES TERRIBLE, AND

THAT TOMORROW YOU ARE NOT GOING TO
SMOKE.

Those are the six main rules. Will you keep
your end of the bargain? Will you try them?
Maybe they sound strange to you. Maybe you
mistrust psychology and psychologists. But try
them anyway.

Remember, at the start we made a gentleman's agreement.

We said: Read this book, put its precepts
into practice, and we guarantee that you will
give up smoking. Or you get your money
back.

We're ready to live up to our half of the
bargain.

Finish the book, do what it says, and, if it
fails, you get your money and no questions
asked.

But—do what it says! That is up to you.

You've been told about the preparations you
should make before you give up smoking.
You've been told six important rules that will
help you to carry out your resolve.

All we ask from you is that you do it. Never mind whether you think the rules sound
peculiar. Put them into practice. You owe us
(and yourself) that much.

Go through the preliminaries. Pick your

time. Then use the six rules honestly and sincerely.

Do that, and, if you really want to give up smoking, you're as good as done with it.

The time is not necessarily right now. Nor tomorrow. Nor the next day.

But it's coming, sure as fate.

7

Some extra helps

THE six rules contained in the preceding chapter are possibly the most important advice you will read in this book. That is why we ask you to study them and religiously put them into practice.

However, there are some lesser ideas and suggestions which can also be of help. Hence this chapter.

One of these ideas is that to give up a bad habit you must substitute a good one. Which is why we are so insistent that you get mints or gum and otherwise pamper yourself and your appetites as soon as you stop smoking. It isn't that either eating candy or chewing gum is a particularly healthful activity, but both are far more healthful and less habit-forming than smoking.

More important, however, is for you to come to a realization of *why* you smoke. Go back for a moment and review Chapter 4 if you don't remember it clearly.

Remind yourself that smoking is an antidote for what is usually described as "nervousness," and that while the times we live in could fairly be described as the Great Age of Anxiety, it is a little silly to give way to worry and fear to the extent that you have to take thirty to fifty nervousness antidotes every day—and more on unusually demanding days! It is far healthier to think a bit about what makes you feel jittery, and do something about *that,* than to drug your senses and numb your nerves with toxic smoke in a meaningless effort to escape.

Once you stop, you will begin to learn, from the occasions when you are especially tempted to smoke, what circumstances, experiences, or people make you nervous. With that realization will also come an understanding of *why* they do.

And when you know that, you will have learned a great deal about yourself. You will be less inclined to seek the small and temporary escape of tobacco than to attempt to solve whatever personal problem it is that makes you "nervous." You'll be well on your way to a permanent cure from the tobacco habit, and you'll be a far healthier person, mentally and physically.

Several chapters back, we asked you to make a list of all the undesirable aspects of tobacco's use that you could think of. We hope you did that. If you didn't, you will begin one immediately, please. That's part of the bargain.

Because now we will remind you that your list is something that goes into your wallet or pocketbook as the time approaches for you to cast off the tobacco habit and enter on the critical first phase of your campaign to give up smoking.

So be sure to:

USE YOUR LIST

Once the day arrives when you step out, for the first time in years, without cigarette or cigar, carry that list with you and consult it often. Consult it *before* occasions when you think you will particularly experience the urge to smoke. Consult it when you are unexpectedly tempted, and read it thoughtfully to remind yourself of the way tobacco really tasted to you and bothered you when you were indulging yourself in it without limit. Consider what each of tobacco's unpleasantnesses meant to you. Read it also during leisure moments when you are not especially tempted to go back to smoking—when you are merely waiting for someone or are riding on bus or train or in a taxi.

Remember, that list is your own report to yourself on what tobacco meant to you in the way of discomfort, inconvenience, expense, coughs, harsh throats, and bad tastes. Use it without fail, particularly during the first week.

Then:

USE YOUR SENSE OF HUMOR

A sense of humor is one of those desirable human qualities that everyone prides himself on having. Not all people have one. How about you? If you do have a sense of humor, use it! Remind yourself how ridiculous it is for an adult human being to let himself become so dependent, not on food or drink, clothing, shelter, or any of the essentials of life, but on one small, tobacco-filled paper tube, that he feels he simply cannot get along without it.

Laugh at yourself a little.

Laugh at the whole thing. True, you won't always be able to summon a very hearty laugh, especially at first. But if you preserve your balance to the point where you can occasionally grin at yourself and your temporary discomfort, even wryly, you'll find the going much easier than if you let yourself grow solemnly melancholy.

Next:

> TALK TO YOUR FRIENDS ABOUT YOUR HAVING GIVEN UP SMOKING AND OF THE BENEFITS THAT HAVE RESULTED.

From the very first day you will begin to notice them. You'll be nervous and jittery at first, of course. But you will also feel more energetic, more alert, sleep better, and enjoy your food more. As time passes, these benefits will increase, and the nervousness will decline.

So when someone asks you how it feels to stop smoking, tell them, admitting the unpleasant parts but also emphasizing the pleasant ones. Whatever you do, don't let yourself get into the habit of self-pity or go into long laments about your sufferings. You're not going to suffer as much or as long as you think. But if you start wailing and grousing about what you're doing, you will talk not others but yourself right out of your own good intentions.

That is because you are your own best sales-man.

One other important point: We have con-stantly emphasized that the best way to give up smoking is to wait for the strategic moment when the best possible conditions prevail. But we have also pointed out that waiting too long for that strategic moment can destroy all the momentum and enthusiasm you have accumu-lated. Therefore:

> IF AN OPPORTUNITY DOESN'T PRE-SENT ITSELF WITHIN REASONABLE TIME, TAKE THE INITIATIVE AND CREATE ONE!

A long holiday weekend can be a splendid time to begin.

If a particularly quiet season for your busi-ness is coming along, when life will be fairly simple and uncomplicated, that can be a good time to begin.

But you can create such opportunities your-self, even if one does not naturally come along. When you have finished this book, made your list, and thought about the rules in the last chapter and the suggestions in this, pick a convenient night to go to bed early. Read for a while, listen to the radio, or do anything else that is quiet and relaxing. Don't smoke while you do this, and turn the light out early. Get a good night's rest. Put Rule Six about controlled sleep into effect on this night; give it just a brief try.

Next morning, when you awaken refreshed, tell yourself that this is the day you begin— and go to it!

Go to it even without the vacation or business lull or whatever it is that you think would best help you on your way. It is fine if you can start with their added advantage. But it is better to start without them than never to start at all.

And the difference in difficulties will not be so great but that you can succeed if you follow these instructions sincerely, honestly, and faithfully.

We have scarcely touched on one great help in giving up the smoking habit: the knowledge, which you will gain as you go along, that you *can* do it. Above all the physical pleasures which non-smoking brings to the long-time smoker is the sudden sense of freedom, and independence, and self-assurance that results from simply going a half day, and then a day, and then two days without any tobacco.

That is a sharp and continuing pleasure,

and every minute you live with it helps to strengthen you against the next minute's temptation. Those temptations will be hard and painful, but the knowledge that you are winning a battle is a wonderful panacea against the aches and pains of the wounds incurred in that battle.

And above and beyond that pleasant, heartening knowledge is the awareness that you are doing something which you will be proud of—not to mention healthier and happier for—during the rest of your life. Six months or six years from now, when someone offers you a cigarette, you will refuse it, but not weakly or defensively through fear of being thought a less-than-regular fellow. You will say, "Thanks—I used to smoke two packs a day, but I gave it up." And you will be looked at with a glimpse of wistful envy, like a freshman looking at a senior who has been through the mill.

One last suggestion:

USE THIS BOOK!

Especially during the first trying few days, go back to it evenings or mornings or whenever you find it most convenient.

Read a snatch here and there, reviewing the

rules, skimming through the opening chapters, refreshing your memory of its facts. For the first week or so, make it your bible. If you do, at each reading you will find things in it you did not notice before, because they did not apply to you so closely at that time.

You will realize, more than ever, that smoking is an irritating problem to a great many people and that in your own lonely battle to give it up you are not alone. Many, many others have felt the same way and still do. And they have won the battle, even though they are less well equipped than you to fight it.

Consult the book often, use your list and your sense of humor, and remind yourself, in conversations with friends, of the benefits you have gained. Follow—once more!—the six rules.

And when the first day, and then the first several days, and finally the first week are over—even though you will still be tempted for a long time to come, see for yourself whether you really want to go back to the slavery of tobacco.

Some pitfalls will still lie in wait for you. We'll consider those in the next chapter. But they are not so hard to avoid once you have fought your way through the first week.

8

And now you are on your way

IF you have done what we asked in the last two chapters, you are now ready to give up smoking.

We are not going to repeat any of the injunctions again, except perhaps one: If you have accepted our guarantee in good faith, which is the way we made it, it is now up to you also to act in good faith. That is, to obey the rules laid down and to do your best—your genuine best—to carry them out.

Ahead of you lies a wonderful experience, the experience of freeing yourself from a burden, of breaking a bad habit, of rediscovering that you are your own boss. It won't come without effort. But if you will make the effort, you'll win.

You will win even though you will first go through some difficult days (don't fear them, but simply prepare for them!), and you will occasionally find yourself face to face with the danger of the unexpected.

What we mean is this: Most smokers have rather fixed ideas about the occasions when a smoke tastes best. They are inclined to tell themselves that they could really cut down or virtually give up smoking entirely except for some few favorite occasions. The first cigarette after breakfast, perhaps, or the one with a cocktail before dinner. Or the comfortable cigar after a hearty and profitable business lunch.

When you stop smoking you will find that the temptation to smoke on these special occasions is actually no stronger than on many others (although you will have to stop in order to find that out).

However, you will also find that the desire to smoke, developed and nurtured by many years of unrestrained indulgence, has become a very insidious thing indeed, and that it has a way of jumping out at you almost overpoweringly, like a strong-arm artist on a dark street, at the most unexpected moments.

You may presently find that the greatest temptations come to you at the very moments which not only are least predictable but seem to be least reasonable. You will be sitting back engrossed in a good movie. Or lying in bed only drowsily awake on a Sunday morning. Or taking a cold, brisk shower. No sense in wanting a smoke then. Yet that is when it comes, so sharply insistent that you almost start automatically fumbling for a cigarette.

Almost, but not quite. You will catch yourself; don't worry about it. And, if you only hold out for a moment, that sudden strong temptation will die almost as quickly as it arose. Just postpone it for a little. Remind yourself that to smoke now is an act of ignominious retreat, after fighting and winning the worst of the battle. And that by now, were you to light a cigarette, the first puff would tell you how treacherously deceitful is the thought that one lungful of cigarette smoke would be fragrant and soothing. Actually it would taste harsh and bitter, and, if you inhaled deeply, would probably make you cough.

Look out, too, for false pride. People who succeed in ridding themselves of a long-indulged, tenacious habit like smoking have reason to be proud of themselves. But don't let yourself get so cocky that you think you can safely smoke just one cigarette "to see what it seems like now" or to demonstrate how you have mastered the old habit.

You can't, and so don't try it.

Even six months after you have given up smoking completely, you can't afford to take that risk, no matter how glibly and convincingly you tell yourself that it is for experimental or demonstration purposes only.

One will lead to another, as sure as you are alive. The first one will taste terrible, and you will laugh at it and wonder how you ever let yourself be enslaved by so noxious a habit. You'll be glad to put it out, and you'll say you certainly don't want any more.

But presently you will light another, maybe an hour or a day later. And presently another.

That'll be all, brother.

The only pride to which you are rightfully entitled is in not smoking at all, and the only way to achieve it is *not to smoke, period*. Not a puff, not a couple of drags, not "just one for the heck of it." *Nothing* in the way of tobacco. For if you have been a heavy smoker, you are far weaker than you think.

Indulge yourself in anything else, not only at first but weeks afterward, if occasion requires. Have a drink, take a walk, eat a mint, go to a movie, buy yourself a new hat or necktie—do anything, but don't give in to the desire, ever so microscopically, to actively inhale tobacco smoke.

As you beat it back, that desire will weaken and attack you less frequently. But it will be there for a long time, and occasionally the old reasons for smoking will present themselves with seemingly new vigor and conviction.

Thus it will occasionally occur to you that burning tobacco is really a pretty fragrant thing. Or that using it is a smart and sophisticated gesture. Or that by now you are its master and therefore have learned to use it in moderation—control it, in other words.

Don't let yourself kid yourself.

If you could afford to try just one cigarette (which you can't), you would find it tasted harsh, gaseous, and overpoweringly poisonous, but you wouldn't stop at one.

If you paused to think, you would know from your own experience that smoking is not smart or sophisticated but a slowly and painfully acquired habit which, once fastened on you, *compels* you to smoke even when you do not want to.

And if you had had more experience with giving up smoking, you would know that very, very few heavy smokers can "control" or confine their smoking to the small amount that is in no way harmful to one's general well-being.

Whatever you do, don't feel self-conscious about giving up smoking! There is no reason why you should, but, if you do, simply say nothing about what you are doing and make carrying matches a custom. Do that, and no one will notice that you do not smoke. The only thing your friends demand of you is that you have a light for them when they need it.

There is one last possibility to discuss, and it is a hideous one. It is that, after giving up smoking and taking the worst that this can offer for a few days or a week, you will, in a moment of utter weakness, slip back into the old ways and light a cigarette.

A hideous thought indeed, and perhaps it is better if we do not even consider the possibility. Certainly you should do everything you can, by postponement and by frequent reference to this book, to make it impossible.

But it might happen.

If it does, there is only one thing for you to do, one thing to think about.

The steeplechase rider who is thrown immediately gets on his feet and mounts another horse, to keep his nerve. The airplane pilot who crashes immediately takes up another plane, for the same reason.

If, after getting off to a good start, you momentarily weaken and yield to the temptation to smoke—think only of putting a stop to it before you lose your nerve. Don't give up weakly, abandon hope, and start smoking again. Recognize that this is the biggest test of all and determine to win it. Don't smoke any more— and if that hurts, worse than ever, bear in mind that you are making up for your lapse.

Tell yourself that you can still win and, by deliberately courting temptation and repulsing it, ride another horse, so to speak. Take up another plane.

If you do, at the end of the day you'll be prouder than ever of yourself and firmer than ever in your resolution.

9

You take it from here

AS FAR as you are concerned at the present moment, this is the last chapter in the book.

There is one more, actually, but please do not read it now.

It was especially designed for the time, soon to come in one way or another, when you embark on the great experiment. It consists of a sort of diary which you should read one day at a time and which will give you some idea of what to expect during the first critical period when you give up smoking. It contains day-by-day advice and day-by-day warnings.

There is no necessity, we hope, for saying that it cannot prove one hundred percent accurate for every case. We cannot promise that you will experience the identical sensations, difficulties, and triumphs in every twenty-four hours that others have experienced. We do think, though, that by and large you will find it an accurate prognosis of your case, and that if you read the first day's entry on the first day, the second entry on the second day, and *do not read on ahead* (although you can *re-read* as much as you like), you will find it of genuine help.

We'd like also to bring up one last but important point.

This book started out with a guarantee, and we have purposely referred to it throughout because it is an honest guarantee. Anything of the sort is remarkably rare in the history of book publishing.

But we have ventured to guarantee this book because we believe two things. One is that there are too many people in this country who smoke too much and who deeply want to give it up. The second is that the principles contained herein are sound and substantiated psychological precepts, and that if they are faithfully put into practice by someone who really wants to stop smoking—as stated in the original terms of the guarantee—such a person will be able to stop.

That statement is based on many facts, not the least of which is our own experience and the experience of many others.

The whole point is: Do you want to give up smoking? If you do, then make sure you have equipped yourself with all the help to be found in Chapters 6 and 7. Write that list. Pick your time—or create it. And follow the rules.

Consult the book often during the first few days and read the daily entries in the next chapter.

Do these things honestly and sincerely and see what happens.

How long does the guarantee last?

That's really up to you. It lasts as long as you really desire not to smoke.

If you have been a fairly heavy smoker for some years, then you are probably going to find that a year after you stop, you will occasionally be seized by brief and inexplicable longings to smoke. And you can't fairly claim to have conquered the smoking habit until those longings end for good and all.

The thing you must remember is that as long as that tendency persists, you must use the knowledge you have gained from this book to combat it and to extinguish the last dying embers of the tobacco habit.

When you have gone without tobacco for six months or a year, you can fairly claim to have won the battle. You will really have won it before then. But whether you retain the victory is up to you, and no guarantee or anything else can retain it for you.

Whether you do is your responsibility entirely. By that time the fight will be over, and what will remain will be at most a kind of psychological mopping-up operation. And the principles that enabled you to win the war will enable you to do the mopping up without difficulty.

But *you* must do it.

You must do it in the same way that you must cooperate in carrying out the various steps of the guarantee. You must do it out of your own sense of honesty and fair play—not merely to us but to yourself. Because you know that you want to stop smoking, that you should, and—now—that you can.

When you have, spread the word. Let other people know that it can be done, that you did it, and tell them the way in which you did it. Because it's a word worth spreading.

And if you'd like to drop us a line telling us how it worked out for you, we'd like very much to hear from you, for there's nothing more interesting to a person who's beaten the smoking habit than to learn how others did it.

Good luck!

10

Day by day

WHAT follows is a synthesis of the daily notes made by the author during various experiments in abstention from smoking. Making the usual allowances for individual differences, it will give the new abstainer some idea of what to expect.

It should be read only one day at a time.

FIRST DAY

You will have a great feeling of excitement, a kind of adventurous feeling. You will be constantly tempted to smoke, but the knowledge that you are doing something revolutionary for yourself will carry you through. You will feel a bit overemotional and perhaps—today or tomorrow—will begin boring your friends with talk about what it means to go four or six or eight waking hours without smoking.

That's fine. Keep telling them, whether they like it or not. You're engaged in a major project, and you have the right to take a few liberties.

Your lunch today will taste as it hasn't for a long time, and so will your dinner. And if you have a cocktail before dinner, it will taste good and the effect will be pleasant. But not like before. Because you will not have worn yourself out and destroyed a lot of your energy by depressing your nervous system. You won't feel you need the drink to restore your strength. It will merely be a pleasure.

SECOND DAY

In some respects this day will be a little easier. You will have the experience of one day's trials and temptations behind you, and the knowledge that you licked them. At the same time you may become aware that you laugh more easily and at less funny things, you get mad or irritated more easily. The normal emotions which your smoking kept under wraps are now beginning to emerge.

Don't let that bother you. Before, you occasionally became irritated or otherwise emotional, too, and for less healthy reasons. This will presently pass, not to return. In the meantime, you may feel a little uncomfortable about your short temper. Just bear your temporary failing in mind, check it as much as you can, and don't worry about it.

Occasionally your hand will stray unconsciously to cigarette box or pocket for a cigarette. When you realize that you can't have it, you will feel a pang. Sweep this out of your mind as fast as you can by thinking of something else.

Remember that by tonight you will have gone two days without smoking, longer than you have gone tobacco-less in—how many years?

And with two days won, you are well on your way.

Don't forget about controlled sleep. Use it tonight without fail.

THIRD DAY

You ought to feel pretty proud of yourself today. You're really rolling! And it won't hurt to let people know how you feel.

How to **Stop Smoking**

One thing you may find hard to explain is the enlarged sense of time, time to do things and the energy with which to do them. And the sense of freedom. You've been noticing smells more, too, haven't you? Your physique is beginning to get rid of the load of nicotine and other poisons that it has carried for years.

If you lit a cigarette now (don't!) it would taste horrible. Believe us, that's true. We know. But don't try it, because even though it did, you would in all likelihood light another after a while. And you've done too much and are going too well to risk anything.

Matter of fact, today you'll probably notice that the smoking of others does not bother you nearly as much as it did during the first few hours of the first day. Right?

Keep on eating mints, or chewing gum, or eating favorite foods, at least for a while. You're saving money in another way, you know.

FOURTH DAY

Better look out, about here.

You've been doing fine and winning victory after victory. But somewhere about now a crisis can come up—it may be some small personal difficulty, or perhaps the Urge to Smoke's big counterattack—that will make things tough.

Be on your guard against this. Don't permit it to make you give in, even a little.

You are already over the biggest hump. From now on there may be other crises, but things will get slowly, steadily easier, and even the crises will be smaller. Think about this today: You are not going to let yourself slip back into smoking, regardless of what else you may do. Too much is at stake. You've invested a lot in this gamble, and you can't help but win—if you don't pull out.

Instead, deliberately tempt yourself with tobacco, in one of the ways suggested earlier, and then thumb your nose at temptation.

FIFTH DAY

Your first enthusiasm may begin to wear thin about now.

You started out not thinking you could do it, and yet you have, and here it is the fifth day. By now non-smoking may have become rather familiar. Not that you're not still tempted to smoke—and often! But the early pride and sense of discovery are getting a little stale.

And perhaps you are getting a little hard to live with. The constant renunciation of temptation can be hard on the nerves. And when your nerves have been under attack long enough, your temper can grow a little short with your wife, friends, children, or subordinates.

Try to watch it, without worrying too much about it. Whatever you do, don't let it drive you to smoking one cigarette or even inhaling one puff of a cigarette. Read over that list and try to reconstruct just how it was when you smoked—the constant pulling down of your energy and resolution and self-respect by *having* to light a cigarette which never really gave you satisfaction.

This may be the most subtly difficult day in the whole critical first week. So if you find things getting on your nerves, simply remind yourself of that and remember that tomorrow won't be so bad. Whatever else happens, if your temper or a sudden bit of anger get the better of you—don't let shame drive you back into smoking again!

Instead, be proud that you have gone as far as you have, for you have a right to be proud—well we know it. And remind yourself that the worst is over, because it is. We know that, too.

SIXTH DAY

Either today or tomorrow you deserve something especially pleasant.

Tomorrow night you will complete a week of non-smoking. That's something!

So right about now you are entitled to a sort of treat. You are entitled to a day or night of fun, of release, of perhaps a little genteel hell-raising.

See that you get it. It may consist of simply going to a movie you've wanted to see. Maybe, if you are the type, it can be going to a night spot and staying up late. (If you are, don't worry about losing a few hours' sleep, because you've got more pep and endurance now than you've had in a long, long time.)

Maybe it's just a new dress you want, or some books, or a day at the beach, or a new sport shirt, or a new putter. But stop and think for a moment of some treat you have wanted for a while and then—get it for yourself! And tell yourself that you've won this because you are now completing a really tough week—and you *are* going to complete it!

Tell yourself that in the morning, and at night, and several times during the day.

SEVENTH DAY

This is a real anniversary for you. It marks the end of your first week as a non-smoker.

Some nervousness still plagues you—and occasionally you still want very much to smoke. Very much.

But stop and think back a moment. How do you feel today in comparison with the first or second day? You've won a lot of victories over the smoking habit since then. The little, sudden desires to smoke still come, but they are easier to repel than they were before. You're far more accustomed to being with other people who smoke, and much more used to the little periods of uncertainty or indecision when it would be awfully, awfully comfortable to have a cigarette.

Considering the progress you've made (which you once thought you could never make), how do you think it will be another week from now? Tougher? You know better.

The very worst is over. It will still be bad occasionally. But not as bad as it has been. And the sudden release of energy which manifested itself in unusual nervous activity, overemotionalism, or sudden tempers—that's getting under control, too. You're beginning to adjust physically to normal, tobacco-less living.

The fight isn't over, but from here on it gets easier. So please determine to get through the next week; and to help yourself, review the chapters on rules, follow those rules, and read your list.

EIGHTH DAY

You're starting your second week now, the second and easier half of the two weeks' period which will determine whether you have given up smoking for good or are going to let yourself slip back into the abyss from which you have so painfully and courageously crawled.

There's a danger to watch out for today and all week. It is that you've now had a week's experience with the pleasures of not smoking. Those pleasures have been marred (more than a little!) by the insistent, slowly dying desire to smoke, and as time goes on the pleasures will increase and deepen, and the desire will lessen. But already the pleasure of being free from the tobacco habit has grown somewhat familiar to you, and whether you realize it or not, you are accepting it a little too easily.

Don't do it! Go over your list again and recall to yourself all the unpleasant things you have now eliminated from your life. Don't take this new well-being for granted. It is greater than you think, and it is worth exercising all your vigilance to preserve.

NINTH DAY

Don't get careless, like an overconfident baseball pitcher who has almost completed pitching a no-hit game and so starts throwing easy ones contemptuously to the batter.

The batter you're pitching against is a very tough fellow. It is a habit which has grown to great strength and wiliness over the years, and it is yet capable of making sudden onslaughts on your new but still young strength.

So be sure you follow the six rules every day. Don't let yourself get bored with them. You need them, and they can still make your task a lot easier.

And, whatever you do, don't try "just one puff to see what it tastes like."

TENTH DAY

Although things are getting under control, today you can expect some strong and sudden temptations, all the more dangerous because you are getting used to non-smoking.

It is psychologically impossible for you to bear in mind at all times the good things that have resulted from giving up smoking. And as time passes, the temptation to smoke will come more unexpectedly because less frequently, attacking from unusual quarters and at unpredictable times. And with greater strength because of that very unexpectedness.

You can counteract this by deliberately courting temptation once or twice a day and by deliberately reviewing the newer, brighter, healthier world which you have now discovered for yourself.

Please do that today and tomorrow and throughout the rest of this fourteen-day period.

It is not that the battle against tobacco will end at midnight on the fourteenth day. You know better. But just as the first week represented the decisive battle in your own little personal war, so this week represents the next most important. Get through them both and, if you continue to use our precepts (and after two weeks you won't have to try so hard), you will have virtually won your fight.

ELEVENTH DAY

This is a day on which you could usefully search out the friends who told you that you couldn't give up smoking and make them eat their words. Don't think we're urging you to be vengeful. But make it a point today to remind at least one and preferably several friends that you have succeeded in stopping smoking. Just think! You have gone without tobacco's gas attack for eleven days. Tell them how much better you feel, and remind them that you have done what they said you couldn't do.

And if they reply that you surely will succumb to temptation sooner or later, tell them that you know all about temptation and are prepared to battle it today, tomorrow, or three months from now.

By doing this you will not only strengthen your own purpose but you will put yourself in a position which is going to recall itself to you when the next major temptation to smoke comes. That is, you will think twice before you let yourself prove your slightly envious friends' contention that it is impossible for you to give up smoking.

Please do this today without fail.

How are you feeling, by the way? Sleeping better? Eating better? Feeling healthier?

How long is it since you woke up coughing and half-asphyxiated from yesterday's two packs of cigarettes or fifteen cigars?

TWELFTH DAY

We've told you before—and now how well you
know it!—that the urge to smoke dies slowly
and can still attack insidiously long after you
have gotten over the worst of it. So watch yourself today. Today or tomorrow it is likely that
circumstances, or simply the physical craving
for nicotine's nerve-depressant properties, will
throw another major temptation at you. That
is, another crisis may be due.

Since you have beaten back everything that
tobacco can offer, you may expect it to try a
new, subtler strategy—fanciful, perhaps, but
fundamentally true. One thing you may expect,
for example, is a little wave of self-pity.

You'll think: after all, look what you've giv-
en up. Why aren't you entitled to smoke like
other people? Why should you deprive yourself
of this innocent pleasure? Why make a mar-
tyr of yourself?

And so forth and so on.

They are silly arguments, really, and if you'll
just think back to some of the early chapters
in this book and cast your mind's eye over
that list of yours for a moment, you will realize how silly they are.

The trouble is that when temptation comes

in that melancholy, self-pitying guise, you may not think back to all the evils you have escaped by stopping smoking. You may not remember that the smokers whom you now are suddenly envying are not "free to smoke" at all. They are prisoners of the tobacco habit. They *can't* stop. You have.

So, for heaven's sake, before your emotions engulf you too completely, please go back to Chapters 3 and 4 and reread them. Give yourself a break, before you jump back into the mess you have just escaped.

THIRTEENTH DAY

Just one special point today.

Wherever you are, or whatever you do, make it a point to take a long, hard look at a tobacco counter.

Look at all the packs of cigarettes, the boxes of cigars, the neat stacks of pipe tobacco.

Look long and hard, then thumb your nose at them and laugh to yourself.

FOURTEENTH DAY

How about it?

Today you complete the fourteenth day of non-smoking.

You've won your fight now. Not that you shouldn't continue after today using all the knowledge you've gained. Of course you should. And it won't be hard because you've had fourteen days of practice. Fourteen tough days. But you got through them.

You're entitled to another big treat now, so give it to yourself. Figure out what you've saved by not smoking for these last two weeks. Then think of how much more, not in money but in general health and pride and everyday living pleasure, you have saved—gained, really.

You're over the big hump at last. You've made us live up to our guarantee, and we've made you stop smoking. Fair enough?

Maintain your vigilance from now on, of course.

Keep the book around and skim through it occasionally. But by now you know how to handle temptation. Just don't forget that knowledge and don't forget to use it.

You're no longer a smoker. You've given up smoking.

You can darned well be proud of yourself. Stay that way.

The End—Practically!

Postscript

THAT WAS where we went out, some few years back.

But in the meantime we have received a lot of rather wonderful mail from readers—wonderful because it answers many questions we have wondered about, and most of all because it proves that the book works. We have wondered, for example, whether this system for stopping smoking can work as well for the extremely heavy smoker as for the normal-heavy smoker. (The answer is: it does.) We have wondered whether it works as well for the young as the old (it does), and for women as for men (yes), and for any particular classes (the mail seems to come mainly from intelligent, sensitive people in the better professions and good economic levels. We've heard from legislators, brokers, lawyers and priests, housewives, newspaper editors and teachers, government employees, servicemen, and women authors.)

Doctors, especially, have used the book for themselves and for their patients. We know of one physician who had a heavy-smoking patient with a serious catarrhal condition. Nothing the doctor could say or prescribe stopped the patient from steadily making his own illness worse by heavy smoking. Finally the doctor tried a neat stratagem: he cleared all reading matter from his waiting room whenever this patient was due to visit him, except for the book that you are holding. With nothing else to read, the patient picked up the book. The doctor purposely kept him waiting for a while to give him a chance to read. In a few "treatments" the patient stopped smoking.

This book has had other unpredictable results. A proper lady we know complained to us good-humoredly—well, *fairly* good humoredly—that she had wanted to quit smoking and that HTSS had enabled her to do so, but that now, every day around 4 P.M., she was assailed by a desperate need to smash something.

Personal counseling is simply something we cannot supply to a constantly expanding audience. But her husband was a good friend, so we sent her a prescription in the form of a half dozen cheap plates and a hammer. For three days she broke a plate regularly at 4 P.M. in her office, smashing it to bits on a newspaper spread on her desk. Thus she came to recognize how childish it all was—not the plate-breaking, but the 4 P.M. syndrome. And in that recognition she was cured of smoking.

Quite a different problem came to light with a long-distance phone call to the publisher of this book in New York City from a lady in Colorado. She feared she could not stop smoking and was considering suicide. Would the publisher get us to call her collect?

We made the call with trepidation for, contrary to a widely held but erroneous belief, people who threaten or even talk about suicide are not just "taking it out in talk." They often try to kill themselves. Not infrequently, they succeed.

The lady herself answered the phone. She was indeed alive, happy, and sounded in good health. She didn't really want to kill herself, she said, but she was worried. She had stopped smoking three years before after reading our book, stayed "clean" two years, and then slipped back. Once again she had stopped and hadn't smoked for some six months, but was afraid she was again about to resume. What could we tell her? We told her what we could —it's already in the book—and we parted friends. She thus became one more incident in the growing body of stories and even jokes about smoking and those who give it up.

Such jokes comprise a new school of humor, if we may digress a moment. There is the *Punch* cartoon, for example, showing an automobile salesman displaying the features of a new car to a prospective customer. "And of course it has the latest safety devices such as seat-belts and no cigarette lighter."

And the one about the man who read so many news stories about the dreadful effects of smoking cigarettes that he finally gave up —reading.

Or the four-packs-a-day man who grew so nervous about the effects of smoking on his health that he went up to nine packs a day.

And the drawing of the young lovers out for a walk and glaring at each other as she snaps at him: "Don't take your withdrawal symptoms out on *me!*"

In real life there is an advertising friend of ours whom non-smoking made so irritable that after three days of him his wife pushed a cigarette between his lips, yelling "Smoke, you son of a bitch, smoke!"

Real life can in fact always top the fiction of joke or cartoon. A news item of a few years back told of the congratulations tendered to America's heavy smokers by a noted Russian scientist visiting Washington, D.C. Their homes would never be burglarized and they themselves would never grow old, he said —"because the smoker stays up all night coughing, and he won't live long enough to enjoy old age."

But let's get back to the mail.

One thing we had wondered about especially and which the mail answered was whether we had overstated the case, and whether other people have been made as uncomfortable as we were by the smoking habit. In that respect replies have been especially gratifying, as you will see if you care to look over our shoulder and read some of the letters (one of which, from a Chicago lady, began: "You darling! I could hug you."). And it's worth your while because some of the readers have suggested ideas they discovered for themselves that can be very helpful.

So just take a glance at some of our mail, please, and learn what some other people have done. The first letter is from a New Yorker:

In another ten days I'll be sixty-four years of age. I started smoking when I was in high school, nearly fifty years ago.

A year ago I was a chain cigarette smoker. At least two packs of king size a day, and another pack if I went out for the evening. Always an early riser, what seemed to bother me most was that I generally smoked seven or eight cigarettes before breakfast.

Then I read the ad about your book. What could I lose? I sent for a copy. I mulled over it for two or three weeks. Then, one day, I decided to quit. It was January 15, 1954. This Saturday it'll be a full year since I smoked a cigarette, cigar, pipe, or "anything." During the year, I haven't broken my resolution *once*.

I thought you might like to have the little card I carried with me for a number of months, listing the objectionable things about smoking that I had overcome. Here it is.

I am deeply grateful to you.

And would you like to see the list this gentleman sent? Here it is:

Burns — suit, furniture, sheets, shirts
Ashes — all over everything

How to Stop Smoking

    Tobacco — in pockets
    Cough — constant
    Sinus — constant
    Smell — little
    Taste — little
    Pulse — fast
    Arteries — constricted
    Tongue — yellow
    Nose — dry
    Expense — at least 50¢ daily

A much different suggestion from a Fort Lauderdale lady:

I found chewing on whole cloves was very satisfying, as I am not a gum chewer and do not like the sweetness of mints. Also, a pinch of salt on the tongue helped a great deal. Maybe these will help others too.

We received this one from Kenya:

I did in fact resort to one little gimmick which I found most helpful. I ruled off fourteen columns of twenty-four lines each on a sheet of double foolscap, and marked off one square for each hour of "non-smoking." This was absurdly helpful. Somehow I got quite keen on filling the sheet, and when the desire to smoke really bothered me I managed to take a collector's pride in adding one more marked square to my sheet.

A lady in San Diego had several ideas:

I found that when I desired a cigarette I would take three large, deep breaths and the desire would leave sometimes for maybe fifteen minutes to an hour, and each day without a cigarette the time would be longer. As each desire arose I would repeat this and found it to be quite helpful.

Also, I found that by drinking a glass of cold water my desire for a cigarette was quenched. It gave me the feeling that all the nicotine in my system was being washed out and the coldness seemed like clear fresh oxygen. Since very few people drink their eight glasses of water a day, this is solving two problems in helping to regain good health. It worked for me and I am sure others will find it to be useful, especially those who do not want mints, gum and other things that may not be to their liking or do not have them around when they need them.

Sometimes the letters are inordinately flattering, and we have edited out all we could. But these first two, from Lincolnton, N.C., and Runnemede, N.J., respectively, were a little hard to edit:

Dear Mr. Brean:
Thank you. Thank you. Thank you.
I feel great.
Thank you.

Except for the signature, that was all.

Another letter-writer broke into verse:

HOW TO STOP SMOKING ISN'T HARD TO DO
IT'S REALLY, FULLY UP TO YOU
READ THIS BOOK, AND WHEN YOU'RE THROUGH
YOU'LL BE CURED LIKE I WAS TOO. . . .
NO MORE LIGHTING MATCHES, OR INHALING NICOTINE
YOU'LL HAVE TO READ THIS BOOK, AND SEE WHAT I MEAN
NEVER AGAIN WILL YOUR LUNGS BE CLOGGED, SMOKING IS FOR THE BIRDS

"YOU *CAN* STOP SMOKING" ARE VERY, VERY TRUE WORDS.

This New Yorker was equally—at least!—expressive, but on another aspect of stopping smoking. He wrote in part:

> Back, now, to the medical profession. Those sanctified bastards are not informed. Probably no profession demands and gets as much respect from laymen like myself. But they do more harm than good.
>
> Any doctor who tells a sick patient (or well one) to *cut down* on smoking is so badly informed that he would do his patient a greater service by keeping his simple mouth shut. A doctor who tells a patient to *stop* without telling him how is doing him no service.
>
> It should be illegal for a doctor to advise a patient to stop smoking without handing him a copy of your book while the words are still in his breath.

This one from a charming friend of long standing came as a complete surprise and is quoted *in toto,* although the first sentence we simply refuse to explain because that would dull the effect.

> Dear Mr. Brean:
>
> If you are the same Herbert Brean who proposed to me in 1949, the answer is "yes." "How to Stop Smoking" shook the camel off my back. You have my undying gratitude.
>
> Gratefully yours,
Gypsy Rose Lee
>
> P.S. I was a two pack smoker!! This is my ninth day but *I'm sure*.

And this is from another Lee letter written the following year:

> I'm still not smoking and the weight is back to normal—it really is uphill all the way, isn't it? But by God, it's worth it!

This one is from a Virginia man:

> I know that I will never smoke again, thanks to you—and I will be willing to sign any kind of testimonial you may wish.

From a Navy technician at a California missile center:

I'm only twenty now, but I had been smoking steadily since I was eleven years old, which represents almost half my life. I haven't touched another cigarette since [reading your book] and, believe me, it's pretty hard to quit when you're in service and 99 guys out of 100 smoke.

From a good-humored priest in St. Louis:

I did it; after twenty-three years of smoking and never being able to stop, I will complete my fourteenth day of non-smoking today.

Nobody seems very impressed but me. It seems to be taken for granted that a priest can and should control his smoking pleasure; I couldn't and had to admit it. Your book and a month of practice did it. So thank you very much for sharing your knowledge of all the angles with me.

From a California housewife:

A year ago today I quit smoking with the help of your wonderful book.

I had smoked since I was twenty-five years old—I am now fifty-six. My husband's record of smoking was about the same. He also stopped a few days after I did.

This one came from São Paulo, Brazil:

For more than thirty years I was a smoker. I did not smoke when I was asleep, but in the meantime I "enjoyed" thirty to forty cigarettes plus ten to twelve thin cigars a day, adding several pipefuls of tobacco each night, seeming never to get enough.

When I saw your book in the book stall, I was skeptical because I had often enough tried to give up, in vain. But I bought it, put it away on the bookshelf, feeling a little better for the try. When I went on vacation a few months later, I remembered and took it along. God bless that day!

From a Beverly Hills broker:

I have averaged six packages of cigarettes a day for thirty-five years. This comes to well over 1.5 million cigarettes. Whether you would say that I was a chain smoker or just a very heavy indulger, at least people like myself are in a different category from persons who smoke forty to fifty cigarettes a day.

I can't begin to tell you how much better I am feeling already, and I know I am only in the beginning of it. If you at any time would like any reactions from a former "six packs a day guy," be sure and let me know.

From a man in Michigan:

I bought your book although I did not expect any good to come of it, except perhaps to laugh at your silly guarantee of money back. But now that I don't really need the book any more (I've quit smoking) I wouldn't take $5 for it unless I could get another. I have smoked for sixty years, since I was nine years old, and have tried several times to quit but unsuccessfully. You have my congratulations and my deep-felt thanks.

From a man in Switzerland:

I have just broken a fifteen-year two-packs-a-day cigarette habit with the help of your book. It is six years since the book was first published . . . and I'm sure the author will be glad to know that after all this time his book is still bringing half-dead people back to life, not only in the United States but in other countries too.

How to **Stop Smoking**

From a New Jersey man:

Thanks a million for holding my hands while I went through the trial of stopping smoking. I've conquered a habit I never dreamed I could control, let alone master. I'm the envy of my close friends.

Sometimes there is unexpected humor in the mail. There was the young Marine who wrote us from Parris Island that he had never smoked in his life until he read this book, and that the first chapter made it sound so inviting he took up the habit, and felt very grateful for the introduction to this new pleasure. And there was this letter from a respected Chicago attorney:

February 7, 1957, marked two years since, early one morning, I read your book. And that same day marked two years since I have quit smoking.

I decided to write you today, as I bought my third or fourth copy of your book with which to persuade others to hit the sawdust trail.

Never felt worse in my life.

Thank you very much.

We've been deeply gratified by the number of persons who wrote us to underline the *pleasures* they had discovered in non-smoking. From Battle Creek, Michigan:

I had almost forgotten the pleasures of non-smoking until last Sunday and since. The very first day I was aware of a tremendous increase in energy, a better appetite and a feeling of well-being. And all the pangs of wanting a smoke are more than compensated for by my having lost that perpetual gagging feeling in my throat that has given me a "nauseated" outlook on life for some time.

I want to thank you for your almost personal guidance as lent me by your book. It is tough to "go it alone" and your book offers understanding and help at a difficult time.

And from Watertown, Massachusetts:

It is far *less* painful than I imagined to really once and for all quit.

Giving up smoking did something psychological here:

Accomplishing the job not only frees

one's self from the effects of tobacco, but also just gives you self-confidence in knowing a hard job can be done.

We could never have predicted that the book would affect housekeeping! But—

> Since quitting cigarettes I feel better, I have more energy, I *sleep* better and wake up refreshed. Also, for some reason, I keep myself and my house neater. All the nice things you describe in your book are happening.

Here is a really dramatic letter, date-lined Laguna Beach:

> I am writing you on the night of my seventh day of not smoking. I am fifty-two years of age and have smoked three packs a day for years.
>
> I had developed a cough so bad that it caused me to give up the best selling job I ever had last year. Also to give up almost all social activities. A week ago my writing was so choky you would find it hard to read.
>
> Miracle! My cough is entirely gone

and the shaking is going. I feel ten years younger and have a brand-new lease on life. I bought and read your book over a month ago and though I followed directions I couldn't believe your book would work for me. But it did and I am certain it is for all time. The release is simply tremendous and what hasn't it done for my self-respect! I couldn't even quit when doctors told me to.

This lady lives in Ohio:

I had been having indigestion, and although I went to three doctors, not one recommended I quit smoking or suggested that smoking contributed to my discomfort. However, in my own mind, I felt if I could give up smoking I would feel better.

You induced me to quit and I can never thank you enough. I didn't taper off—I just said to myself: Tuesday (*why* that day I don't know) I will quit; and I did. That was three months ago. I got rid of the indigestion after the first week and have been able to eat anything from that time on. Incidentally, I had been smoking continuously for twenty-one years— am forty-four years old.

From Indianapolis:

> I have a feeling of great elation at "not *having* to smoke."

But, as we said, some readers have ideas of their own about how to stop smoking, and some of them are darned sound. They may tend to be a little more individual than those you have been reading, and thus more limited in scope, but they can help. For example, there was one man who wrote us: "You left out one good way to discourage yourself from smoking. When I stopped, I made it a practice always to have a big ashtray full of ashes and cigar and cigarette butts, left by friends, on my desk. Whenever I was tempted to smoke I just leaned over and inhaled a great lungful of that awful, dead smell. It immediately convinced me that I did not want a cigarette."

The same method, but with a decidedly reverse twist, was suggested by a Kent, Washington, gentleman who kept an opened package of cigarettes at hand and smelled it at least twice a day, wafting the bouquet under his very nose and then stoutly putting the pack down, contents intact.

A New York newspaperman had this thought:

A great many smokers are afraid to go off cigarettes because they feel that "when I drink, I have to smoke." I found that it is completely possible to drink without smoking. I noticed, too, that one of the strongest factors in luring me to cigarettes, after I had been off them for about ten days, was curiosity. It might be good to warn your reader not to get so curious that he thinks he can get away with "just one."

Here's a Spokane lady's idea:

It has been over two years. I've regained my health, never felt better in my life, have much more energy, and wouldn't take up smoking again for anything!

My copy of your book shows considerable signs of wear and tear, since I carried it, a package of cigarettes, and my lighter at all times for the first three weeks. When the gnawing desire for a cigarette began (which at first seemed to be every five seconds), I fished out the book first, and read all about the evils of the weed, and the pep talks, and consulted my list pasted to the cover. Sometimes it took several readings to get the message across—but, as you predicted, it was only one battle at a time.

Here are a New Englander's (New Hampshire) ideas:

I read the book, called it hogwash, and wistfully wished I could stop smoking. A couple of weeks later I reread the book and decided perhaps some day I might try to quit smoking; and one day, just as you predicted, I said "This is the day" and stopped. That was over three months ago, and I can truly say I've broken the habit —but I'm not even thinking of trying to smoke to see how it tastes. I would not dare, even though I have no desire to smoke. I followed your suggestions and added a couple of ideas of my own that helped me a lot, and these ideas I'm passing on to you in case you're interested:

1. I figured out my smoking cost me 45¢ a day plus a little extra for matches, flints, lighter fluid, etc. Every night I put 45¢ into a jar on the shelf and watched it grow. Occasionally I tossed in an extra dime for flints, etc.

2. Each night I pasted a silver star

on the calendar and got a big kick out
of seeing the rows of stars grow. Also,
I would have been very much ashamed
to have had to break the line of stars.
These two simple things proved to be
of great aid to me in my fight against
smoking.

And, to present all sides, you may be interested in this idea from Alexandria, Virginia:

On only one point I take issue with
your book, but I think it is a very important point. At least for me, your advice
as to the circumstances under which to
"take the plunge" is diametrically op-
posed to all my experience. The better
I felt, the more I craved tobacco—and
conversely. Who wants to smoke when
seasick? Or suffering from a bad cold?
Or a hangover? I'm sure I never did.
Those unhappy times were the ideal times
for me to swear off—when the mere
thought of a smoke was nauseating.

Maybe there was method in your
choice of the *toughest* time to make the
break—possibly on the reasoning that all
subsequent craving would theoretically be

of lesser intensity—but personally I prefer to *ease* into the battle little by little.

And from Twenty-Nine Palms, California:

I am not sure I am right but am quite confident that a person who wants a drink of liquor or wants to smoke will find the desire gone if he will suck on an orange. Possibly you already know that I am mistaken; if so, no harm done by this suggestion. But if you do not know that I am wrong, you might like to investigate. I think the effect lasts only as long as the taste remains.

This gentleman lives in Alberta, Canada:

Just a note to tell you that after eight years of smoking, I have finally quit, thanks to your book. I might add that it was necessary for me to rip out and destroy your first two chapters, since they increase the temptation to smoke.

And this from an Indianian:

When I read your book and came to the part about the list, I thought it wouldn't be very effective. I did make one, however, because of the deal we had made. That list proved to be one of the biggest factors in helping me to give up smoking. Here is one reason, which is also my suggestion.

I made the list with *two* columns: one headed with a minus sign, the other with a plus sign. Under the minus sign I wrote, as you suggested, all the things I didn't like about smoking. Under the plus sign I included all the things I liked or expected to enjoy about not smoking, and added to this list daily as new pleasures presented themselves. I included everything I could think of, from the fact that my wife would be pleased, to not having to go to the dentist as often to have my teeth cleaned. As the days went by, the "plus" list grew, and consequently so did its ability to help me in my new venture.

This is just a small suggestion. Quite possibly you won't like it. But I thought that just in case you did and wanted to include it in your next publication, my writing to you was the least I could do to show my appreciation for your having helped me to break a habit I thought was going to enslave me for the rest of my life.

I know that this idea more than doubled the effect of the list in my case. I should like to think it can do the same for others.

To change the subject a little once more, here's a letter that is almost a Hollywood movie scenario. It came, however, from Lawton, Oklahoma:

It had been in the back of my mind to stop, but last August I had a greater motivation than ever. My husband was in Vietnam, had been there since January, and wasn't due home until the next January. It used to bother me when he kissed me to think that the taste of stale tobacco might be offensive to him. . . .

So I decided to try your book and make an effort to give up cigarettes before he came home. According to you, I could hardly have chosen a worse time. In addition to the fact that my husband was in a dangerous part of the world and I was under constant strain from worrying about him, I suddenly developed motherin-law trouble and my own father stopped speaking to me as well!! But my desire to stop smoking was strong, and the trying situations were not going to stop me from at least making an effort.

So, with the help of your book, I stopped smoking on August 15th of last year, and I haven't smoked since. It was my intention to save the surprise for my husband, when he came home, but in the meantime he wrote and asked me if I would like an ivory cigarette holder and matching case. The last temptation!!

I wrote him no, and told him why. He was delighted. He got me a topaz instead.

When we came here to live (near Fort Sill) we needed a wall unit in which to put our tape recorder, multiplex, turntable, TV, bar, stereo speakers, and books. We were lucky enough to find what we wanted.

The day it was finally gotten in place, filled with books and all the other things it was designed for, we sat opposite it and admired it and complimented each other on our excellent taste! I did some rapid mathematics and came up with the interesting fact that our lovely new piece of furniture represented about eighteen months of cigarette money for the two of us.

So. I not only feel better, sleep better, have more energy, and save money. But I also have the self-satisfaction of having broken an unnecessary and probably dangerous habit. And that's the most important thing of all,

Thank you very much.

This came from Medway, Massachusetts:

Nearly *thirteen* years ago (March 10th, 1952) I stopped smoking. I had smoked 2 to 3 packs a day. I enjoyed it and had no intention of stopping. I knew I smoked too much and tried to cut down with no success. One day I saw your book in a bookstore in Harvard Square. The money-back guarantee intrigued me and I intended to test it out. To my amazement and that of my family and friends—I stopped smoking and have never desired to resume the unpleasant habit. Recently I bought a new copy of your book (I gave the old one away) and I intend to leave it around the house hoping that my smoking friends will borrow it. . . .

I shall always be grateful. Your book changed my life in a very positive manner.

And on April Fools Day-plus-one in Ferndale, Michigan:

I bought your priceless book "How to Stop Smoking" on April 1. On April 2 at 5 P.M. while watching my meal cook, I started to read while smoking a cigarette. Miraculously, that was my last cigarette, even before I made the list and followed your instructions.

Now, six months later, I am very, very grateful.

A Vancouver, B. C., man wrote:

I have bought five or six of these books and have shipped them to some friends of mine at no cost to them. Three of them quit the habit and two of them are still on trial, but they are trying. Any time I have a chance to help another man to leave this habit behind, let me assure you that I will go out of my way to help, even if I have to buy the next dozen books.

Perhaps after all these accounts of hard-fought and sometimes almost-lost battles, it is only fair that we provide you with a couple of off-beat anecdotes that may well keep you on the straight and narrow for a long, long time. Here is the first:

Not so long ago we sat at lunch next to a pleasant lady who immediately established her perspicacity and good taste as far as we were concerned by saying she had read this book, liked it, and as a result had stopped smoking. And thereby created a pleasant problem for herself.

She had put on a few pounds as a result and so, as a second result, had presently gone on a diet and taken them off. But the ease with which she had done this led her to go on dieting and finally her husband had complained that she looked like a high-fashion model instead of the girl he had married. Now she was happily engaged in restoring some of the lost weight and dug into the sole Normande with enthusiasm. And she looked great.

The second has another kind of message:

There was once a physician who, as is the way with doctors, had a doctor of his own, a personal friend, whom he consulted about his own health. When he was in his late thirties this physician began developing difficulties about the face and jaw, and his doctor-friend told him he should give up the cigars of which he was a heavy smoker.

The physician knew he should, but he was deeply immersed in a fascinating practice and, while he once made it for more than a year, he could not permanently give up smoking. His symptoms grew worse and finally, after many years, ominous. Toward the end he had to prop his diseased jaw open in order to smoke. But smoke he did and he died of cancer of the jaw and mouth.

His name? Sigmund Freud. The man who single-handedly began the revolution in modern psychology and who almost certainly knew more about the human mind's deepest workings than anyone before him could not himself stop smoking.

If by now you have done it, be proud of yourself. You have a right to be. You have outdone Freud himself.

Feel kind of good?

We'd like to know, if you feel like writing.

Keep Up With The BESTSELLERS!